Container Garden[illegible]

Get maximum results with minimal effort by going
Up, Down, & Over!

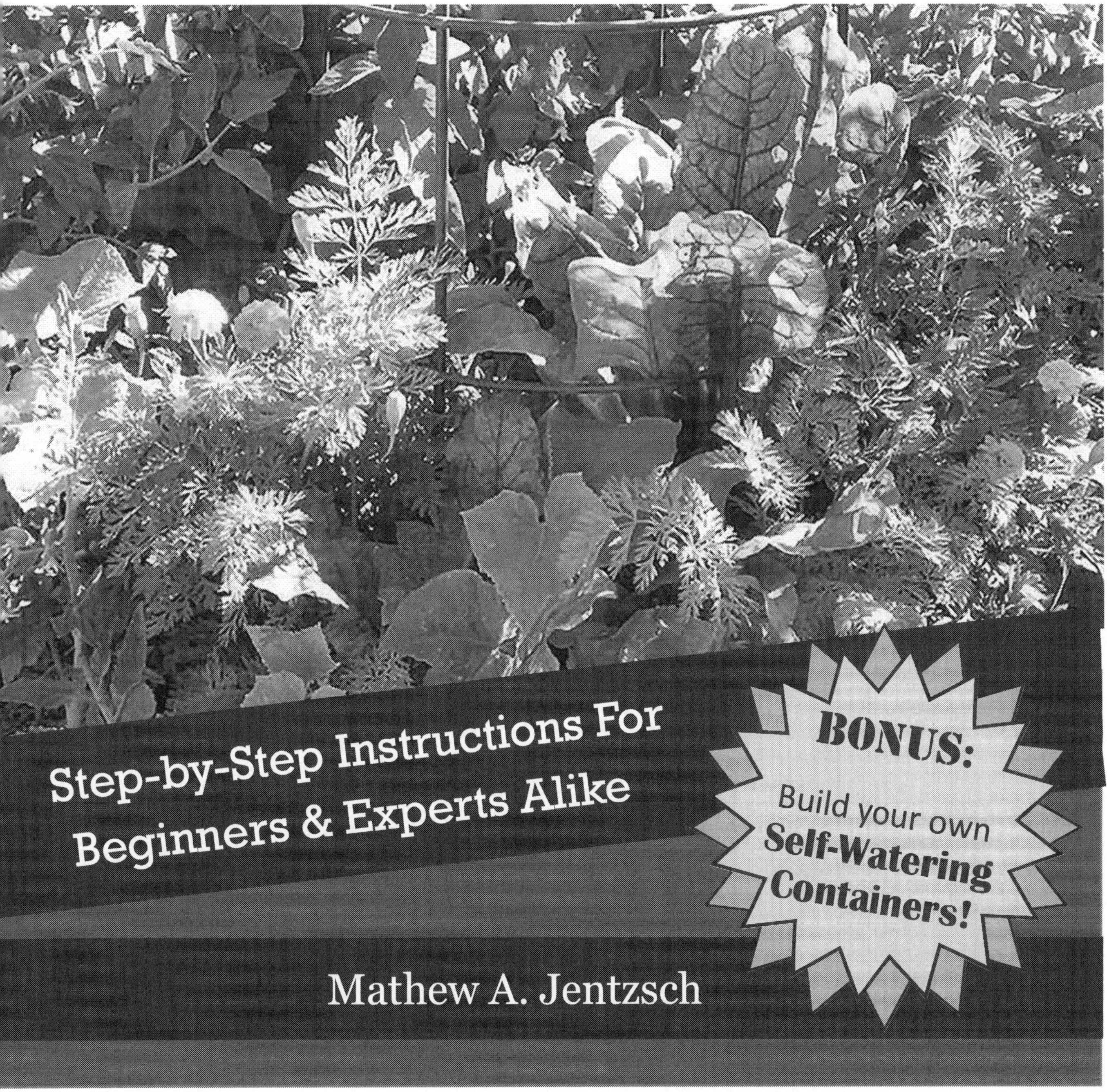

Step-by-Step Instructions For
Beginners & Experts Alike

BONUS:
Build your own
Self-Watering
Containers!

Mathew A. Jentzsch

Copyright

The information contained in this book is for informational purposes only and does not guarantee success by the user. Weather, watering, fertilizing habits, container location, soil choice, and many other factors can contribute to the success or demise of everyday container gardeners.

A portion of the proceeds of this book will be donated to Operation Smile.

Author

Mathew A. Jentzsch

Testimonials

"I have been following this 3D system for planting in containers for over 4 years now. I can plant outside more than 2 months earlier due to the greenhouse effect of the SolarCap®. I have harvested tomatoes off of my plants by the end of July. Normally it is into September before I can enjoy them. I am amazed by how much produce I can get from one container. My best year, I got over 70 lbs. of tomatoes, along with radishes, carrots, spinach and lettuce - all from ONE container! This book is a step by step guide on how to grow the maximum amount of produce in a small space."

Shannon Copeland, Sherwood, Oregon

"Your book, Container Gardening in 3D, *excited me about gardening again this year and for the first time in a long time, even my kids were excited. I only have 1 daughter left at home, and she not only helped me choose* what *to plant, but with the actual planting, watering, and harvesting as well. It was a hoot because I haven't had a kid excited about gardening for a long time now. Gardening in the past meant work...this was fun!*

Stephen Labrum, American Fork, Utah

"Mathew Jentzsch's Container Gardening in 3D *means I don't have to stress my back with endless weeding! Instead of spending a whole day getting the garden planted, we have everything done in about an hour. We get more out of what we plant with a lot less work and use a smaller space!*

Crystal Field, Richland, Washington

"I have lived in apartments for the last 7 years and have never had the space to garden, even in grow boxes. I was introduced to Container Gardening in 3D *and the self watering containers. I have never had so much fun gardening. It is incredibly simple!"*

Aaron Jaussi, Payson, Utah

Acknowledgements

I want to take a moment to thank those who have encouraged me to write this book and have helped me along the way.

First, a big thanks to my dad for instilling in me the gardening bug in the first place and to my mom who encouraged me to just be me.

Second, I wish to thank all family and friends who have been willing to test out my ideas for *Container Gardening in 3D*.

Third, much thanks to Jill Major for being my editorial mentor and Michelle Miller, a good friend who is always willing to be a sounding board for my ideas.

And of course, I have to thank my wife, Mary, who has patiently put up with all of my wild ideas over the years. This one kind of snuck up on us both, but as always, she has been super supportive and encouraging. Love ya, honey!

Foreword

As an avid gardener and professional horticulturist, I have experimented with all types of gardens, both in the ground and in containers. My gardens have been as simple as a few containers on a patio or deck to half acres of vegetables and flowers, planted in lovely neat rows. But as Mathew so aptly points out, long rows of vegetables give rise to an abundance of weeds which need to be dealt with every time the eager gardener turns around! As my children have grown and my back, knees and hips have aged, I garden more in containers and less in the native ground. However, like many of our readers, I planted one tomato per pot or a couple of peppers. It always seemed like quite a waste of space for the amount of available soil in the pot.

Mathew's clear and helpful explanation of his *Container Gardening in 3D* method is so brilliant and yet so elegantly simple, that any gardener can be successful. I have embraced Mathew's system with my containers this year and am extremely pleased with the abundance of vegetables from each pot. If you have ever planted mixed containers of flowers with lovely trailing varieties interspersed with clumping and upright flowering plants, you will wonder why you never thought of the same type of system for your veggies! In addition, he provides practical and helpful explanations of growing media, container type and fertilizer suitable for a beginner or seasoned gardener.

Our increasing interest in locally grown food and healthy eating are excellent reasons to grow your own. When you know what has gone into the container, you can be confident of the quality of what comes out for your family's table. Following Mathew's fail proof method will yield plentiful and healthy produce from your garden with a minimum of effort.

Happy growing!

Michelle L. Miller, M.S.

Horticultural Soil Scientist

Overview

I grew up on a farm - not a big farm mind you, but a farm nonetheless. My parents were hard working folks with not a lot of money, but I never felt poor. There were cows to milk, irrigation pipe to move, and fruit to harvest. With a family of 12 to feed came a really big garden, which entailed the obligatory weeding, watering, weeding, planting, and oh, did I mention weeding? My dad spent many hours tilling the ground with his big Troy Built walk behind rototiller, while my siblings and I spent many an hour cleaning out our barn and hauling the manure/straw mix to our garden plot. Somewhere along the line my dad decided to become more of an organic gardener and before I knew it we were hauling every free organic product he could find into our garden space. This included cleaning out chicken coops and hauling away every rotten hay bale he could find. One haystack was so old it turned out to be one giant mouse nest and believe me when I say, there was a small gray surprise behind almost every bale. I'm not the squeamish type, but when a mouse runs up your arm and jumps off your shoulder, it tends to give you a little bit of a chill. In my youth, I always thought the garden was out of necessity, but as I got older I realized my dad just loved to garden. He was always proud of that first ear of corn or eating tomatoes by July 4th.

Our garden was big and it took a lot of upkeep. One of our least favorite things to do was what we lovingly grew to refer as the "slug patrol". We would get up extra early, take two wooden slats and go slug hunting. Seems the little critters just loved living under all of that hay mulch my dad added to our garden every year and our job was to seek and destroy them by smashing them between the two slats. Think of it as a very medieval mechanical form of slug control.

I did not share my dad's enthusiasm for gardening at the time. To me it meant long hours on my knees either weeding or planting or harvesting. It just meant work. Oh sure, I enjoyed the fruits of the harvest, but it mainly meant more work for me and at that age, work was a four-letter word. Still I did learn a lot about gardening and when it came time to choose a major in college, guess who ended up choosing horticulture? It is a profession in which I gratefully have been involved in one way or another for the past 35 years.

And to think I owe it all to my father. Thanks Dad.

So when I finally got the chance to have my own gardening plot, what do you think I did? Why the same thing I saw my father do: till the ground, make long narrow rows, space out the plants, and water like crazy. I had some success, but I also had lots and lots of failures. Who knew there were so many different weed varieties on the earth? Because I was basically the only weeder, the family garden, which started out with the best of intentions, ended up as one big weed patch with just a few obligatory vegetables thrown in.

As my little family got bigger, and after moving several times, we finally arrived at our current location on about a half acre of ground. It was the perfect size for my future family garden! So what did I end up doing? Again, the same thing I saw my father do! It reminds me of a story about the wife who cuts off the end of the ham and puts it into her baking dish. Her husband sees this and asks her why. She replies, "I don't know, but that is how my mother did it." Her mother came to visit a few days later and the husband asks his mother-in-law, "Why did you cut off the end of the ham?" His mother-in-law replies, "I don't know, but that is how my mother did it." A while later, the grandmother comes to visit and the husband asks, "Why did you cut off the end of the ham?" The grandmother replies, "Because my pan was too small!"

I found myself virtually doing the same thing: repeating over and over what I had seen my father do. As my family got older, I started to lose my helpers, but the garden space remained the same size. Then one year, I was so busy and with no help, the garden did not even get planted. It did however grow a very nice crop of weeds that I mowed once in awhile just to keep them somewhat under control.

That year there was some potting soil sitting around and I decided to put some veggies into a container at the last minute. To my surprise and delight my containers were producing - a lot! The yield was so good I began to wonder what I was doing sweating over the bigger garden when I could do some of the same things so much easier in a container. I had essentially no weeding time and all I had to do was make sure they were watered and properly fertilized. I decided to expand the experiment. The following year I planted several larger containers and involved other family members. It worked. Since then, I have been trying different ideas, mixing and matching different veggies and varying starting times.

I began researching literature that would support this idea and found a few books, but not as many as I thought I would. I was aware of the surge of interest in what is called, *Square Foot Gardening,* but what I was attempting to do was a bit different.

As I read the current literature on gardening one theme began to recur: out of necessity gardening is changing. Small farms are disappearing as more folks either live in the city or in suburbs and even though there are many who want to garden, they don't always have the room to do so. Personally, I began to garden in containers, not because of the lack of space, but because our family's dynamics were changing.

We are all at different levels in life and have different reasons for trying container gardening. No matter the reasons, I know it works. It's fun and a LOT less work. Notice I did not say "NO work," because some effort is involved, but much, much less, which as I grow older I appreciate more and more.

My Container Gardening Motto – *Maximus Containicus Horticus* (MCH)

The basic idea behind this motto is really just this, get all that you can (Maximus) out of your container (Containicus) gardens (Horticus). Meaning push the envelope, not only from what can be grown in a container (selection), but how much, (intensity/density), to what likes to grow together (companion), to how often (succession). The *Container Gardening in 3D* concept pulls all of these principles together. Over the next few chapters, I will discuss some items that may change the way you think about home gardening.

Of course, I realize that those with bigger acreages may not decide to do this, but then I ask myself, "Why wouldn't they?" If you truly like to eat your own produce, what's wrong with starting out in a container early in the spring, then moving out to the regular garden when the ground warms up and can be worked? One can certainly lengthen out the growing season by doing so, thereby enjoying the benefits of the harvest much longer. This system can work whether you live on a large piece of property, in an apartment, a mini house, a condo, a trailer, or even a tent!

Below are some reasons you might want to give this a try regardless of your current growing situation:

- Less watering - *A big deal where water is in high demand and being limited due to regulations.*
- Little to no weeding - *One of my favorite reasons!*
- Locally grown with NO pesticides - *It's your choice.*
- Less overall time required - *I'm busy, aren't you?*
- Less space required - *No room for a traditional or Square Foot Garden? Don't let that stop you!*
- No tilling - *I'm just getting too old for that anymore.*
- Easily accessible - *Put it anywhere on any terrain.*
- Handicap accessible - *With a little help, anyone can do this.*
- Proximity - *Closer to house, which means more likely to be harvested!*
- Mobility - *These can be moved - either around your yard, or to a totally new location.*

And who knows - after doing this for a few seasons, you may decide to replace the garden with turf and ONLY grow in containers. I did.

As Arthur Ashe once said, "Start where you are. Use what you have. Do what you can." So let's get going. As you read through the material, if you have any questions you can email me at *mathewj@containicus.com* or check us out on Facebook under "Containicus".

Watch for these little notes as they appear throughout the book as they may shed some additional "light" on a particular subject. Above all - have fun!

Table of Contents

"Anybody who wants to rule the world should try a garden first."

Old Garden Saying

Chapter 1

The 3D Concept

The Concept

To most people the concept of growing vegetables in containers is represented by the picture to the left; one plant in one container. This is how many folks are introduced to container gardening. The *Container Gardening in 3D* method goes beyond this - way beyond! The goal is to maximize *all* the space allowed.

3D Gardening

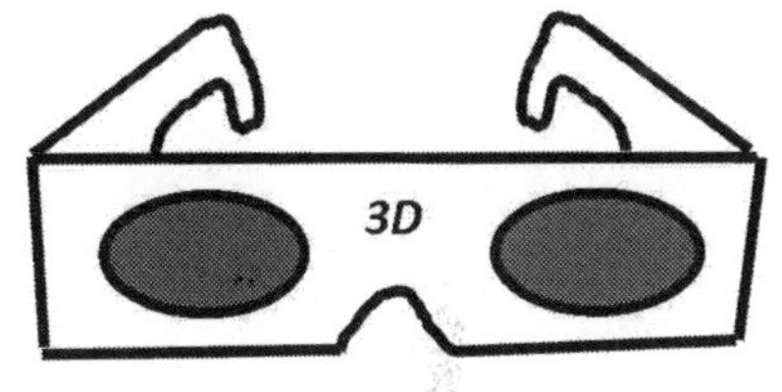

If you are like me you have probably been dragged to one of those movies that hypes itself as 3D. Although it's amazing how much the 3D format can add to a movie, I find the one-size-fits-all glasses give me a headache. I seem to spend half the movie looking through them, then over them, then through them - over and over again just to see if there is any difference. Finally I give up, leave them on, and try to concentrate on the big screen. Luckily, there are no headaches involved with the *Container Gardening in 3D* idea! But just like 3D strives to add to the total movie package, I am asking the same question - what can I do to add more to the container gardening experience and increase possible yields?

Remember the old Star Trek series on TV? Mr. Spock played chess on a board that had 3 different linear space levels. I am trying to do the same with *Container Gardening in 3D* - think three dimensionally. I have so much less space in a typical container than a regular garden I NEED to use all of it. To truly illustrate how I *Container Garden in 3D*, I will be talking about "levels," and "zones." Let's start with levels.

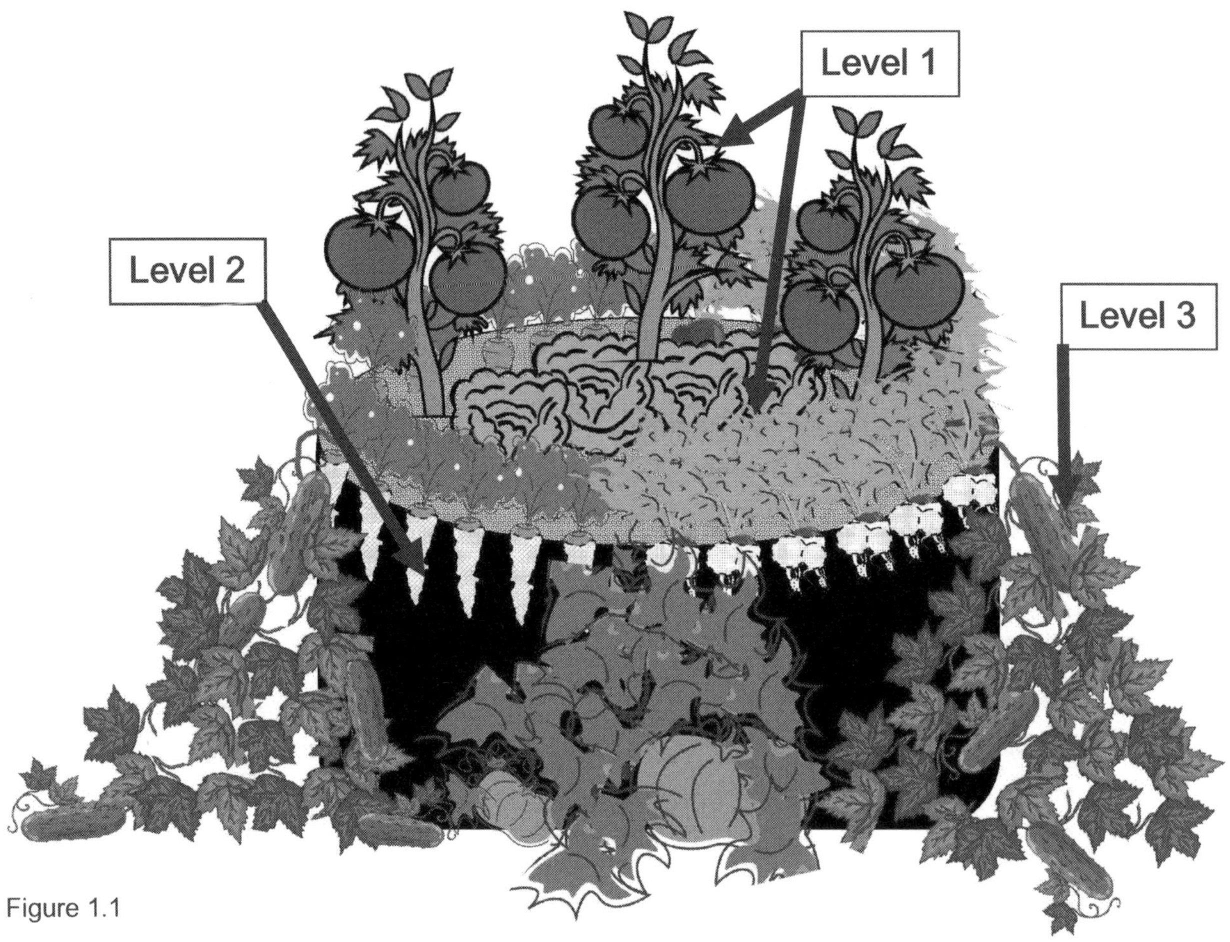

Figure 1.1

Levels

Look at the illustration above (Figure 1.1). Notice how there are 3 different levels. Each level represents a different linear space level just like the 3 different levels on the Star Trek chess board. To put it more simply, each level represents where the produce will be harvested.

Level #1: All cool or warm season plants that grow ***straight Up out*** of the soil, such as tomatoes, peppers, eggplant, spinach, lettuce, swiss chard, peas, etc.

Level #2: All plants (usually cool season) that grow ***Down into*** the soil, such as radishes, carrots, beets, etc.

Level #3: All plants (usually warm season) grown out of the ground that can ***weep Over the edge*** of the container, such as cucumbers, pumpkins, melons, squash, cantaloupe, etc.

It is important to understand these levels as they will determine in large part *where* in the container to place certain plants.

The actual "how to plant" is covered in chapter 5, The How To...Let's Get Dirty!!!, page 45.

Zones

Zones represent where I choose to place the actual vegetable plants inside the container. To better understand how I go about planting my containers, I have created a planting chart. It is important to know that I am not using containers that are only 10 or 14 inches wide. Could you? Sure, but with the bigger size of containers comes more opportunities or options. So I use 21 and 30 inch diameter containers. Those sizes also help in the ease of finding pots, soil packaging, and SolarCaps® (greenhouse-like covers that allow you to start planting earlier in the spring, see chapter 7, Peripherals, page 70).

Since this can be confusing at first, I will go step by step through each zone and when they are planted. The description on how they are actually planted will be covered in chapter 5, The How To...Let's Get Dirty, page 45.

Zone #1 - represented by icons 1A - 1D. See Figure 1.2 & Figure 1.3

Zone #1 represents warm season plants that will be planted when the soil is warmer, later in the spring. Their place is saved by small plastic cups placed *upside down* (see Picture #1). These places are meant for plants that will get quite large and will either grow straight up or weep out over the edge, i.e., tomatoes, peppers, eggplant, cucumbers, melons, etc. (representing levels #1 & #3).

Below are two different planting charts: Figure 1.2 & Figure 1.3. The biggest difference is there are four zone #1 plants in one container and only three in the other. Although they look very

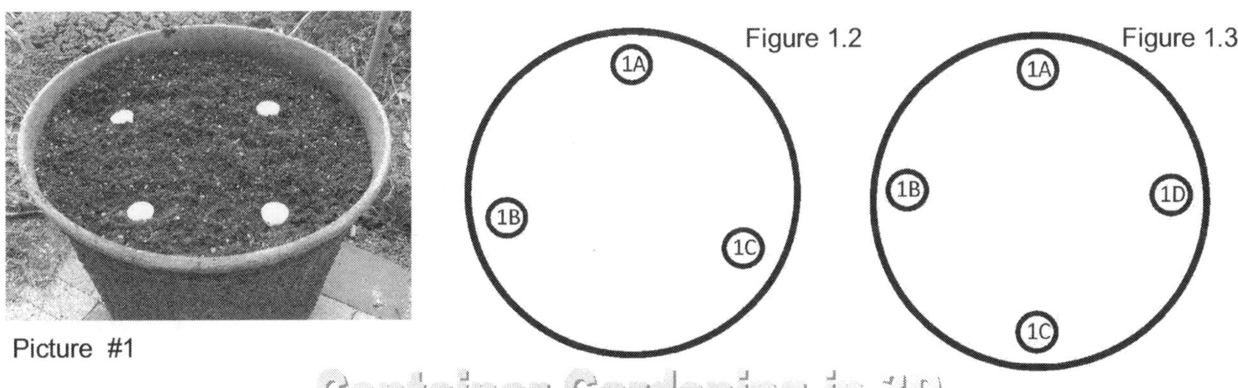

Figure 1.2

Figure 1.3

Picture #1

Figure 1.2 represents a 21 inch diameter container, and Figure 1.3 represents a 30 inch diameter container. The placement of cups will be covered in chapter 5.

similar, they are also very different. I have used both charts for both sizes of containers, so feel free to interchange them or make up your own. Once you understand the concept it is fun to experiment! Going forward, I will only show the container with four zone #1's, but the concept is the same for both.

Note! *IMPORTANT: Zones #2 & #3 are the first two zones planted in the spring!*

Zone #2 - Represented by the ring, with sub-zones represented by 2A - 2D. See Figure 1.4

Zone #2 is actually the very first zone I plant in the very early spring. It is saved for cool season vegetables, plants that can germinate with cooler soil temperatures and withstand frosts. These plants will grow *down* into the soil: i.e. radishes, carrots, beets, etc. It is important to remember that you can do all or just a part of this zone. For example, if you want to spread out your radish harvest, plant sub-zone 2A the first week, plant sub-zone 2B two weeks later, sub-zone 2C two weeks later than that, then finally sub-zone 2D. This will keep your radishes coming on for the next month or so. Or if you want to harvest them all at once then plant all of zone #2. You decide.

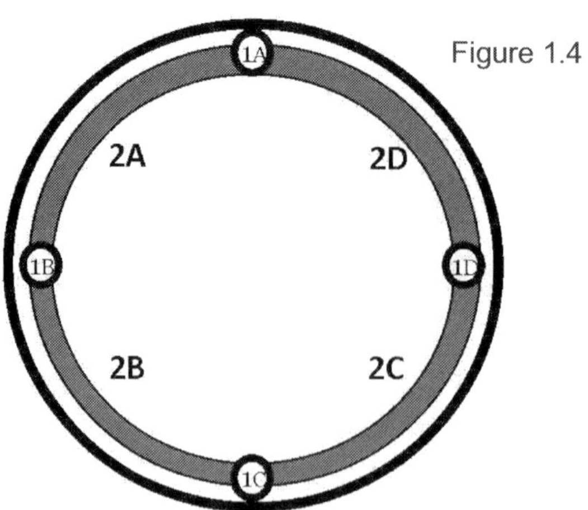

Figure 1.4

Zones #2 & #3 can be interchangeable - meaning you can plant ANY cool season root crops in either zone. Sometimes I mix them up and plant one zone half carrots, and half radishes. Experiment!

Zone #3 - Represented by the inner ring, with sub-zones 3A - 3D. See Figure 1.5.

This Zone is also planted in the early spring with cool season plants, and like zone #2, can be planted all at once or in sections. As mentioned above, I save this zone for items that grow *down* into the soil, not up (level #2). Could you plant other veggies here? Sure, but remember two things: 1) if you grow above ground plants in these two zones you are virtually taking away one of the dimensions available to you: down into the soil, and 2) it will become very, very crowded. But experiment. Try different combinations of cool season vegetables that you enjoy eating and see what works for you.

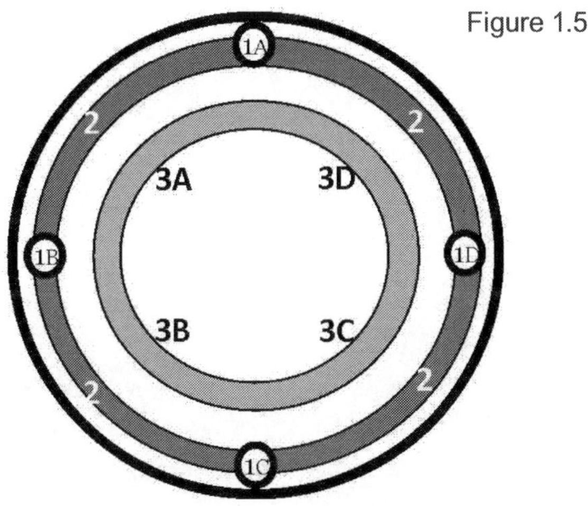

Figure 1.5

Zone #4 - Represented by the dots. See Figure 1.6 & Figure 1.7.

Zone #4 is also planted in the early spring with cool season plants. I save this zone for items that will grow *up* (level #1), usually cool season plants like lettuce, spinach, swiss chard, etc. As shown in Figure 1.6, I often cut this space in half (see dotted line). I plant one half with one kind of vegetable (large dots) then the other half with another (smaller dots, Figure 1.7). This seems to work out quite well.

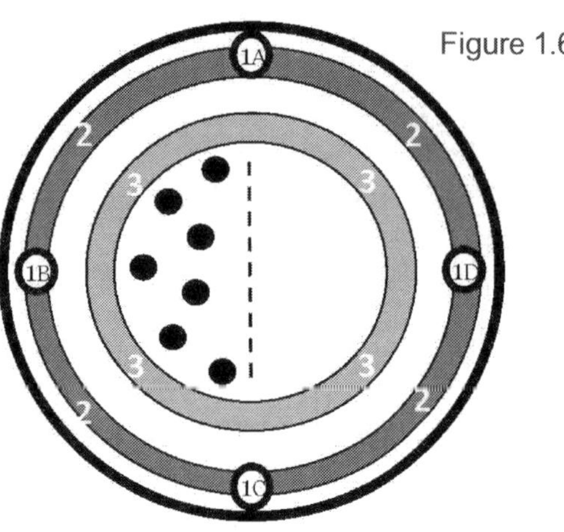

Figure 1.6

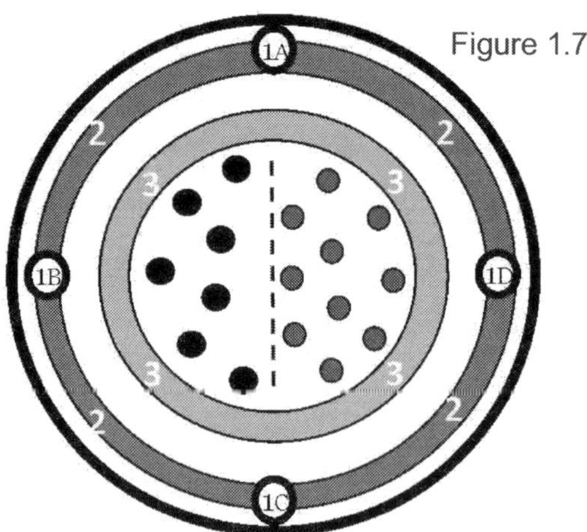

Figure 1.7

The picture below shows an example of a container with zones #2 and #3 planted with it's upside down plastic cups (zone #1) in place. It is now just waiting to have the holes and trenches back filled (covered) with soil.

Example of all 4 Zones

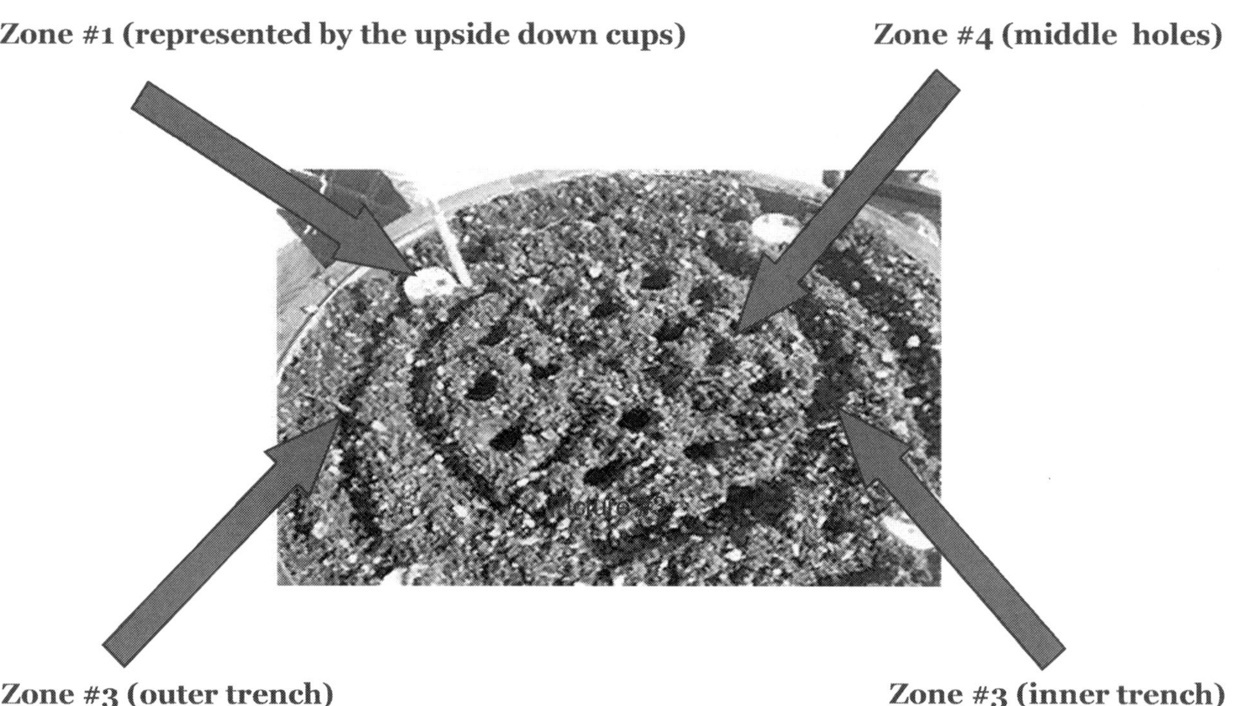

Terms - Intensity/Density, Succession, Companion, Location

Intensity/Density

This is at the heart of reaching our goal of Maximus Containicus Horticus. It's how you get the most out of your container gardening. The idea is to put in as many vegetable plants as you can get away with so you can get as much yield as possible. I know I push the envelope, planting at a much higher rate than recommended. This way many plants can be enjoyed while thinning and some plants can be harvested while others are growing. I like to think of it as *Square Foot Gardening* on steroids!

Succession

It is basically this: while you are harvesting one crop, you are planting the next to be harvested later.

Companion

Just like some people, some plants would rather spend more time together than with others. In her book, *Carrots Love Tomatoes*, author Louise Riotte writes, "Vegetable growers find that companion planting provides many benefits, one of which is protection from pests." Many organic farmers know that marigolds provide some natural resistance to certain pests, as does garlic and onions. Tomatoes not only love carrots, but basil, chives, and parsley. Some argue that radishes grown with lettuce seems to taste better. But by the same token, some plants do not do well together. Louise Riotte states that peppers like a family. I have found this to be true. When put in containers that ONLY have peppers, they thrive. In containers with other plants they don't seem to do as well.

Location

When it comes to successful gardening, it's really a lot like selling real estate: location, location, location! Most garden plants need sun and the most popular ones, like tomatoes and peppers, need lots of it, up to 6 hours per day. So find the place where they will have the best chance of success and it may not be the first place you think of. For example, I know one person who really wanted to have their containers on their back patio. The mixture of veggies and flowers would make a lovely combination for entertaining guests. The amount of available sunlight, however, was poor. The necessary 6 hours was not possible. This person ended up running her pots down her long driveway where the sun was available in maximum quantities and where she was able to run water. Her containers are thriving. So find the best spot and then if you want to have a container where the light is borderline, try one just as an experiment. You may be surprised at how well they do. Or plant some shade loving flowers with cool season veggies in the hot part of the summer.

"A man should never plant a garden larger than his wife can take care of."

T. H. Everett

Chapter 2

Containers

Buy any book on container gardening and they will tell you that you can grow plants or veggies in almost anything and technically that is true (see below). You can grow some nice little veggies in almost any size container. Many folks enjoy having a little herb garden on their window sill or a tomato in a pot out their back door. But in the *Container Gardening in 3D* system, not so much. I want a container that has enough root zone area to support all the veggies I'll be sticking in there, a container that will give me lots of options, and a container that will not dry out too fast during the heat of summer. If you want to grow an herb garden in your window sill by all means do so, but to really get the maximum yield possible, I want something that can handle it.

Gives new meaning to MPH - Mobile Petunias Here!

Which container do you prefer? The Pro's & Con's of each.

Material	Pro's	Con's
Clay	Very ornamental, clay breathes - allows air circulation to roots.	Quite fragile, heavy, and the freeze/thaw cycle can crack the pot over the winter.
Plastic	Inexpensive, light weight, many sizes. Can last a long, long time. Fairly easy to find.	Non-descript, can be hot in summer.
Molded Plastic	Lightweight, weather–resistant containers. Some are more durable than others. You will get what you pay for. All shapes, sizes and designs.	Some will not last long outside. Others are quite expensive comparatively, but will last forever.
Wood	Very attractive. Will need to provide your own drainage holes if whiskey barrel. Can make your own planters to any shape and size.	Heavy, can rot. Treated wood not recommended for growing vegetables.
Pulp	Inexpensive, light weight, offers some insulation to root zone.	Durability. Look for wax seal on bottom and top of containers for extended life of container, otherwise they can rot quickly.
Concrete	Very, very durable. Limited sizes and configurations.	Very heavy.
Grow Bags	Light weight, good air circulation to roots. Fairly inexpensive.	No structure, so soil mass provides all structure. Might be a bit tipsy till plants get established.
Self Watering	Water reservoir will allow longer times between watering.	Must use good soil as some will not wick or will stay *too* moist, which can encourage insects and disease.

Roots go deeper than you think.

I use containers that are at least 21 inches deep and 21 inches wide. As we will discuss, I want a good root system and the ability to push the envelope when it comes to growing in tight quarters. You will need containers that have good drainage holes in the bottom; otherwise, they can be sawed off barrels or fancy clay.

Look at the chart on the left, as it briefly talks about the different materials that containers can be made out of and the pros & cons of each based upon our *Container Gardening in 3D* system. As mentioned above, I am looking at these container options with an eye to successful growing in the whole 3D system. Others will have their own reasons for choosing which material works best for them and you can use just about anything IF it has good drainage holes in the bottom. Unless of course, you are planning to make self watering containers (see below).

If you want to take advantage of the season extending SolarCaps® (see chapter 7, Peripherals, page 70), you will need to make sure the diameter of the container top is 21 inches across. They also need to be circular in nature, otherwise, as we see in the picture at the beginning of this chapter, it's up to your imagination.

Self Watering Containers

If you look online you can watch many "how to" video's on ways to make self watering containers. I have tried several commercial self watering containers and like the way they work. The amount of time I worry about watering these containers is much less than those I hand water. Below is a simple diagram of a self watering system. The reservoir will wick up into the pot as long as there is contact between the water and the soil extending down into it. We will discuss these more in chapter 6, Watering, page 55.

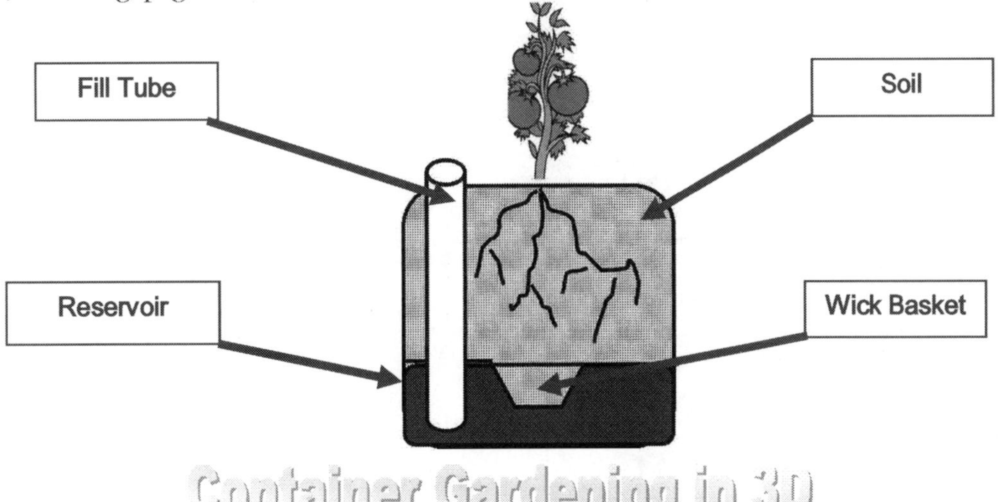

" I love it when you talk dirt!"

Anonymous

Chapter 3

Choosing the Right Soil

When asked what is the most important element to achieve success in container gardens, I always reply with the same answer - the soil. It's a necessary first consideration when talking about container gardening as good soil is the foundation of everything you want to achieve. This is the one area you don't want to do "on the cheap" as it can affect all of the following:

How much water the soil in the container can hold (texture).

How much fertilizer will actually get to the plant (pH & C:N ratio).

How deep the roots will penetrate (porosity & compaction).

All of the above are very important properties of good soil and I will go over each one of them so that you will feel comfortable with these terms. The soil has the ability to work for or against you, so let's jump right in and get our hands dirty (so to speak).

Soil Terminology

To really understand what we are talking about when discussing what works as a container soil, we need to understand some of the options. The following are some of the terms you will hear in today's market place.

Mulches: Mulches are meant to be used as a top dress *on top of* your flower beds as a weed barrier or to help retain moisture in the soil. Typically, mulches are a woody product and are not composted. Mulches are NOT meant to be used in container gardening.

Soil Amendments: Soil amendments should be *incorporated* or tilled into the landscape or garden soil. These types of products may or may not be composted, but are NOT meant to be used in a container.

Garden Soil: This is what we normally think of as dirt. It usually comes into your house on the bottom of your shoes. NEVER use this in your containers. It will not work. You will understand why as we go along.

Compost: Compost can be any organic matter that has been composted over a period of time. The challenge lies in the fact that there are many different ideas out in the market place on what raw materials make a good compost and how long something should be composted before it's ready for use. I define compost as something that has been allowed to decompose over a period of time of at least several months. The time must be long enough that it is no longer "hot" or is still decomposing. The rate of decomposition should have slowed to a point where it has almost stopped.

Potting Soil: This is meant to be used in containers and does not contain any real soil or dirt at all. Usually it is made from combinations of the following raw materials: peat moss, composted bark, perlite, vermiculite, and/or coconut coir. I will get back to this one.

Why the definitions? Because there is much confusion out in the market place and the folks who make all of the above products are not helping things. Many manufacturers are blurring the lines between the definitions to get homeowners to purchase a less quality product at a lower price point. Since there are no consistent definitions from state to state, many manufacturers get away with this tactic. Just remember the old saying, "garbage in, garbage out" works for potting soils as well as it does for computers.

So it begs the question…is there such a thing as the perfect soil?

Sure, and since we are talking specifically about containers, it would look something like the graph in Figure 3.1.

Surprised? The perfect container soil is more than just solid organic matter; it is, in fact, a lot of air and water. These two principle elements (air & water) in the perfect container soil is so important, it is hard to express.

Let's look at how each affect the soil.

Solid Organic Matter

In the garden, the soil is made up of a combination of sand, silt, clay or only one of these. Organic matter is made up of broken down things like grass clippings, wood fiber, leaves, etc., and represents only a small portion of the total soil profile.

In the container, the solid matter is actually not made up of soil, but of other items like peat moss, bark, sawdust, com-

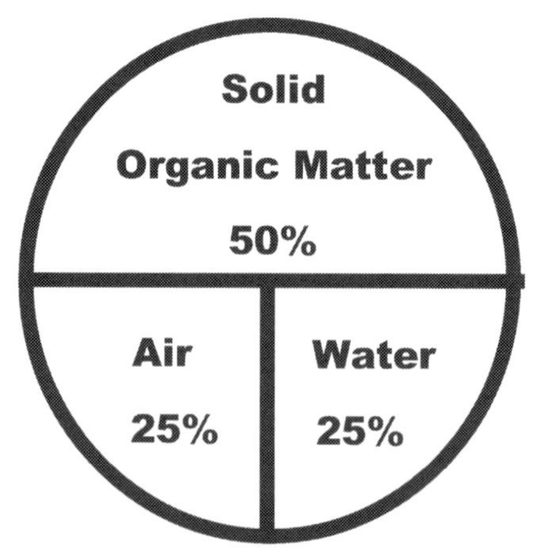

Figure 3.1

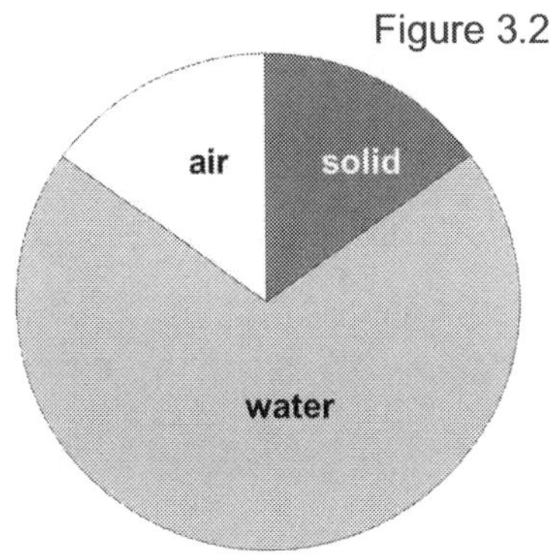

% of air space left after watering.

post, coconut fiber (coir), perlite or vermiculite. Unfortunately, some manufacturers have been known to include raw materials like manure, un-composted compost, wood shavings, broken down wood pallets, etc. A little later on I will take a minute a look at why some of these raw materials can do more harm than good.

Air

As mentioned above, most folks are surprised to see air as an essential part of the soil profile. Indeed there is a constant transition of air molecules that happen between the roots and soil. As Figure 3.2 shows, water will fill up the pore space and take away from the air space. This is okay for brief periods of time, but just like us, plants can suffocate. The porosity of the soil is very, very important. That is why garden soil or dirt makes a very poor soil for containers.

Look at the following pictures.

Picture #1 is a planter at an apartment building where the developer thought he could save money by using garden soil/dirt instead of using a true potting soil. It did not take long for all of the plants in these containers to die. The landscaper had to go back in, dig out all of the dirt, and replace it with a potting soil. Did he save any money? Don't think so. Most garden soils will compact in a container, and once that happens, good-bye to any air movement in that soil! Refer again to Figure 3.1. Look at how important air is to good plant growth in a container. This is why many container soils contain perlite, bark, or other amendments to increase the air porosity.

Now look at the picture on the next page (Picture #2). The landscaper told me that he thought he had enough amendments (meaning big rocks) to make the topsoil work. Nice try, but no. Because the soil had such a heavy clay composition, adding rocks to it only made it more like concrete than a potting soil. The next chart (Figure 3.3), shows how compacted soils and poorly drained soils affect the percentage of air that is allowed into the root zone. Either scenario can be deadly to plants.

Picture #1

Picture #2

Water

It makes sense that the soil must have some water present to help the plant grow optimally, right? Water helps nutrients get into the plant and is needed by cells to do their thing. As you may have noticed, not enough water causes the plant to wilt and eventually die. But on the other hand, too much water will drown the plant or will allow disease pathogens to be present which can also kill the plant.

It's always good to remember the soil as depicted in Figure 3.3 and how much air is in an optimum mix. Obviously, when you water the amount of air will decrease (see Figure 3.2), but that will only be temporary as the plants use the water and some of it evaporates. Of course, you also need to know what tendencies the plant likes; a swamp plant likes a lot of water, while a cactus is equipped to live without hardly any. Lucky for us when it comes to vegetables, most like to have good even moisture.

Your gardening life will be much easier if you understand the relationship plants have with air, water, and soil...represented by the three graphs shown below.

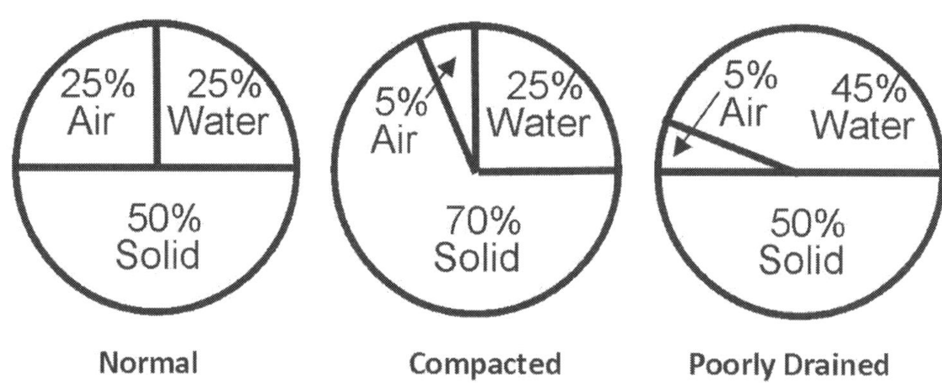

Figure 3.3

Soil Texture

Texture is the soil property used to describe the relative proportions of the size of materials making up the soil. In garden soils this would be talking about the percentages of sand, silt, and clay. Since I am NOT using garden soils in containers, this will be more about the differences in peat moss, bark, coco coir, compost, sawdust, perlite, vermiculite, sand or any other ingredient a soil manufacturer may include in the soil mix. As a general rule the following components exhibit certain characteristics.

Peat Moss (Picture #3)

Peat moss is the number one ingredient found in today's potting soil. Notice I said "potting soil," not soil amendment, or mulch, or top dress, or top soil. Light brown in color, peat moss is a plant material that is harvested mostly in Canada from old bogs that have been drained. It is spongy in nature and works well in containers. Peat moss is a good water holding material, has a very low relative pH, and depending on how long the peat fibers are, can be quite porous. Small fibered peat is very fine, and will hold much more water than long fibered peat. This is why fine peat is used in germinating mixes. The peat you buy in large bales at the store is usually a very fine peat as it is the "cast off" peat from the coarser stuff requested by professional growers. I do not recommended peat alone for container growing, although there have been tests done on peat only mixes. These peats are long fibered and very coarse in nature, and usually only found at professional growers. Peat in a container will begin to compress and will visibly shrink over time.

Picture #3

Bark (Picture #4)

Bark is the part of trees covering the outer trunk. During the milling process the bark is taken off the trees and usually seen as a waste product (much like the fine peat found at retail nurseries and many home improvement stores). Most professional mix companies are very specific about which trees they use bark from, because some have oils or other problems associated with them that can limit plant growth. This is why most barks used in mixes are softwoods, usually either pine or fir.

Picture #4

These barks can be "aged" or "composted." The main reason is that the C:N ratio (pg. 31) needs to be quite low to avoid "nitrogen draw down." Some companies will say their bark is composted, when in reality it is only "aged". They make it look composted by adding elements that darken the outside of the bark. But as you have heard before, "You can't fool Mother Nature." The bark will start composting while in the container and will have negative effects on the plants therein. Try to make sure the bark in your mixes is composted at least 3-4 months. Bark adds stability and drainage to mixes and has a pH value over 7. Bark mixes will have less shrinkage. Bark is not recommended for container growing by itself.

Coco Fiber (Picture #5)

Relatively new in the growing arena is what is called Coco Fiber or just Coir. Coir is the outer husks of coconuts. Once it is removed from the coconut, it is shredded and compressed into bales to be sent to various markets. Coir is an interesting material for growers. It is usually coarser than peat moss and can add some aeration to containers. The unique quality about it is it can also hold a large amount of water. You will find this product in most "water holding" type mixes on the markets these days. Unlike peat moss, it can be coarse and still hold a large amount of water. Coir's pH is relatively neutral. Coir is not recommended for container growing by itself.

Picture #5

Picture #6

Compost (Picture #6)

The word "compost" covers a large field of soil amendments. Usually, this term is used for manure or bark based products that have been composted. The challenge lies with the source of the original material that was composted. Was it pig manure, horse manure, chicken manure, cow manure, spent mushroom compost, human bio-solids, shredded bark, landfill green waste or what? Some composts are great and can be a great addition to garden soils, but because of the potential variability, unless you know exactly where the compost came from and its origins, it can be dangerous to use in a container. For example, if it is a manure based compost, it can be high in salts; not a good thing for container soils. Composts CAN be used by itself in containers if you can vouch for their quality. Do not take the manufacturers word for it either. Composts typically are high in pH, will hold water, and may already come with some nutrients.

Picture #7

Sawdust (Picture #7)

Way down the list of preferred components for mixes is sawdust. Sawdust is usually the white wood of a tree, minus the bark. Sawdust is usually NOT composted so its C:N ratio is around 600:1 with a pH over 8. You may ask why this is used in mixes at all? Some companies who are trying to keep costs low or are meeting a price point will add sawdust as a filler. They may add extra nitrogen to try and make up for the nitrogen draw down, but others may not. Sawdust, by itself, is not recommended for container growing.

Vermiculite (Picture #8)

Picture #8

Vermiculite is an amendment called an aggregate and is popped like popcorn when heated at high temperatures. Tan in color, it is a little more porous than perlite and can hold water and nutrients. For a time, most of the vermiculite that was available in the U.S. was from a mine in Libby, Montana. Unfortunately, it was shown that this mine was also contaminated with asbestos, which caused its closure in 1990. Other sources were found that did not have or carried very low levels of asbestos. If you are concerned about this here are some thoughts.

Pre-mixed soil companies are very aware of this issue and have been looking for sources that contain no asbestos. (Think of the liability exposure if they still used something that contained asbestos). Beyond that, pre-mixes use very little actual vermiculite per cubic foot and are usually moist which will reduce dust. If you are working with straight vermiculite keep it moist to reduce the dust. If you are still unsure then wear a respirator while handling dry vermiculite. Once wet and in the container, the chance of it harming anyone is virtually zero.

Picture #9

Perlite (Picture #9)

Perlite is also an amendment called an aggregate. It is a gray rock that is also heated to an extremely high temperature, but ends up white in color. Very light weight, it works wonders when added to potting soils to help in porosity and drainage. It is easily the most common aggregate found in professional potting mixes. One of its biggest drawbacks is because it is so light weight, perlite will float and can collect in piles. Once it is established, however, it will usually not move.

Zeolite

Zeolite is a mined mineral that has been around for a while. It is used in many different industries like cat litter, deodorants, water purification systems, detergents, and is very prominent in the healthcare industry. It is used in agriculture as well, but sparsely used by the horticultural industry. Due to it's ability to store, then slowly release important items like nitrogen, phosphorous, and water, I highly recommend it for home containers.

You will not find this in any pre-mixed soils that I am aware of so you may need to look around a bit to find it. Use a fine grade material meant for use with soils. Mix one - two pounds per cubic foot of soil. Will plants grow in your containers without zeolite? Sure, but it will certainly raise the chances of success.

Other Soil Concerns

Lets take a moment to talk about some other concerns one needs to know when choosing a good container soil.

Soil pH

It might be more than you want to know, but if you understand how pH affects plants it will help in choosing a good soil for your containers. Without getting too technical, pH is the measure of something that is either acidic, neutral or basic in nature. For example, sulfuric acid would have a very low pH, distilled water would be neutral, and lye would have a basic or high pH. When it comes to plants, would it surprise you that some plants like an acidic soil and others like a soil more basic? Luckily, most plants you will be putting into a container like around the same pH (6.2-6.8). The problem occurs when you have soils or soil amendments that are more acidic or basic than that. For example, peat moss has a pH of around 3.5, and some composts have a pH in the 8s. This may not seem like much, but every 0.1 difference in the numbers is 10 times more one way or the other.

Look at the chart Figure 3.4 on the next page and how it pertains to pH and nutrient availability. As an example of how to read the chart, go down the list till you see the element iron. The graph shows that as the pH gets higher (moves to the right of the graph), the width of the line gets smaller or less available. This basically means that the pH of the soil is limiting how much the plant can take up the element of iron into itself. The iron may actually *be* in the soil, but once the pH starts going past 6 on the scale, it begins to be tied up by the soil and the plant can't get at it, causing the plants to go chlorotic (or experience yellowing, see Picture #10). This is a very real problem that many greenhouse growers deal with on a daily basis. On the other end of the scale is molybdenum. Once the pH gets BELOW 6.5, it's availability starts to diminish. We will discuss this again in Chapter 4 when we discuss fertilizing, as different fertilizers can influence the pH of soilless media.

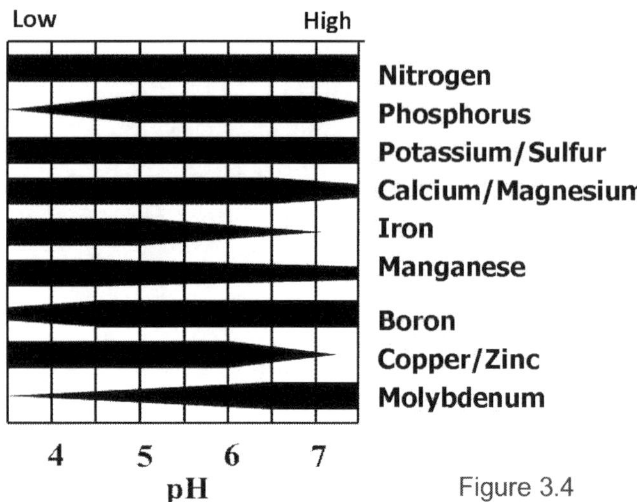

Figure 3.4

Carbon to Nitrogen Ratio (C:N ratio)

I don't want to get too technical here either, but I think it is important to talk about the carbon to nitrogen ratio, hereafter referred to as the C:N ratio. Every soil contains some amount of carbon. As it says in Genesis, "Man is made of dust and to dust shalt he return." There is another old saying, "Ashes to ashes, dust to dust." All living things are carbon based. Upon our death, Mother Nature will use everything at her disposal to break us back down into dust. This same thing is happening in the world of soil 24/7, whether in your garden soil or in the soil in your container. Little microbes break down carbon to make organic matter or humus. This is actually a very good thing, but to do this these microbes need nitrogen to help them do their work. That is one reason why it is recommended to add nitrogen to your compost pile; it aids in the composting process. If there happens to be a shortage of nitrogen, the composting process will slow, but not stop entirely. The little microbes will do everything they can to keep going, even if it means stealing nitrogen away from nearby plants. This process is well known in the greenhouse industry as "nitrogen draw down". It is a major reason why some plants will start turning yellow. Not the same yellow we saw above with iron deficiencies, but yellow none-the-less. (It will begin in the older leaves, and if not corrected, spread through the rest of the plant.)

Picture #10. Petunias are very susceptible to iron chlorosis once the pH gets above 6.5. See how some leaves are a sickly yellow color and the veins are more pronounced on the leaves?

Material	C : N Ratio
Soil Humus	10 : 1
Grass Clippings	19 : 1
Manure (Rotted)	20 : 1
Sphagnum Peat Moss	50 : 1
Leaves	65 : 1
Compost	80 : 1
Coconut Coir	80 : 1
Pine Needles	225 : 1
Bark	500 : 1
Saw Dust	800 : 1

Figure 3.5

So why do *you* need to know this? We've mentioned once before the old saying, "You can't fool Mother Nature." If a product is not truly composted those little microbes will continue to break down the carbon, which as we discussed, takes nitrogen. They will potentially steal nitrogen from any plant growing in that mix. The chart to the right (Figure 3.5) shows the C:N ratio of different materials. The higher the ratio means the more carbon represented and the harder it is to break down; thus more nitrogen will be required to do the job.

Unfortunately, there are many products on the market these days that claim to be compost or composted. You have to ask yourself, "Are they really?" If you choose something that is not truly composted and put it in either your garden or your container, your plants will begin to turn yellow and their growth will be stunted. For example, look at the huge difference between compost and bark. This underlines why it is so important to know if the product you purchase has really been composted for several months or just been aged for a week or two. Our little microbe friends don't care who you are or how much you have paid for this product; their job is to break carbon down and they never fail.

Salts

Another thing to watch out for is a silent killer known as salts. These mostly show up in products that contain some kind of manure as an animal waste product. I have tested some potting soils that contain manure and on a scale of 1 to 10, they were a 13! High salts stop the transfer of water to the root zone so the plant will begin to mimic being under drought stress. Read the label of all your potting mixes. If they contain any kind of manure, whether human (bio solids) or animal, I would stay away from them for container growing, unless you can verify the quality of the source.

Organic vs. Inorganic Soils

After going through the explanation of the raw materials most potting soils consist of it would be easy to think that all potting soils are organic. Many manufacturers use the term "organic" very loosely. Do not be fooled. If this is important to you, you should look for those soils that are

The Organic Materials Review Institute or OMRI acts like the Good Housekeeping Seal of approval for all things organic. Look for their logo to ensure a particular product is truly organic.

either approved organic by the USDA or have the OMRI seal. OMRI stands for the Organic Materials Review Institute. They are basically the Good Housekeeping Seal of approval for all things organic.

Many professional mixes consist of the organic raw materials we have just mentioned, but also contain a synthetic fertilizer charge and wetting agent. If you are not of the organic mind set, these will probably not bother you, but if so, make sure you know EVERYTHING that is in each bag you purchase.

Flashy Trout Back Romaine lettuce - a family favorite. The wine red colors are stunning, and it's so easy to grow!

Q & A

Can I add compost to potting soil to increase the water holding capacity?

Yes, but be aware of the quality of the compost. As I mentioned, some manufactures who claim their products to be composts are not composted at all. This will cause you grief down the road.

Can I add garden soil to the potting soil?

I actually know some professional growers who do this; however, I do not recommend it for the average homeowner for three main reasons: 1) garden soil will bring with it weed seeds; 2) it can also bring disease pathogens; and 3) it can plug up the mix if you get it wrong and reduce the water flow and air porosity. Its not worth the chance. Stay away from anything that can make your soil toxic!

So what should I look for in a good potting soil?

A good potting soil is really a combination of many of the raw materials I've just covered. Here are the components that I look for in a good potting soil and their percentages: Peat moss (40%), coco coir (20%), *composted* bark (20%), perlite (20%), wetting agent, and a starter nutrient charge. If some vermiculite were thrown in (5-10%) as well, that would be okay. The percentages of a mix you actually find in your area may vary, but if you can find a professional blend that matches closely to this mix, you've got it made. If you cannot find something close to this, then I would look for something that is peat moss (50%), coco coir (30%), perlite (20%). In the retail store, examples would be something like Miracle-Gro® Moisture Control potting soil or Black Gold® Water Hold potting soil. If it does not have a starter nutrient charge, that's okay - you will be adding your own anyway.

The most important thing: stay away from high salt, un-composted products, as they will only cause frustration and heart ache down the road. I cannot stress this enough.

Important! Stay away from high salt, un-composted soils!

"Early to bed, early to rise: Work like hell and fertilize"

Emily Whaley

Chapter 4

Fertilizers

The definition of a "complete" fertilizer means it contains the three following elements: nitrogen, phosphorus, and potassium. This is also known as N-P-K. These are considered the macro nutrients necessary for good plant health and growth.

By definition, a fertilizer only needs to contain nitrogen, phosphorus, and potassium to be considered a complete fertilizer. It does not need any additional nutrients.

Macro Nutrients

Nitrogen

When it comes to nutrients, nitrogen is numero uno! It is the nutrient that plants need in the greatest amount. It makes plants 'green', helps the plant grow, and produce chlorophyll. No matter what form the nitrogen starts out as (organic or inorganic, water soluble or pellet), microbes will break down the nitrogen fertilizer into either ammonium or nitrate ions so the plants can uptake it through their roots. Plants starving for nitrogen will steal it from the older leaves to supply it to the younger ones, which will

Picture #1

cause the older leaves to go yellow first and the plants will appear stunted (see Picture #1). Too much nitrogen and plants will put on too much vegetative growth at the expense of the fruit.

Phosphorus

Phosphorus is the second number in the complete fertilizer equation. It helps with rooting, flowering, and proper cell function. Most experts today think we add too much phosphorus in general. That is why many professional fertilizer blends have gone from an N-P-K ratio of 20-20-20 to 20-10-20. Phosphorus deficiencies will show up in the purpling of older leaves. Too much phosphorous can cause the tie up of calcium, which can be a deterrent to proper tomato growth.

Potassium

Potassium helps with cell health and development and protects against diseases. Most experts want a one-to-one ratio with nitrogen. For example: 15-0-15. Deficiencies show up on older leaves; first as a yellowing between the veins then leading to a total leaf yellowing or edge burn.

Secondary Micro Nutrients

Calcium

Calcium helps with the plant cell wall structure, as well as providing transport to other elements. Some veggies need extra calcium. For example, tomatoes are very susceptible to blossom end rot when calcium is in short supply (Picture #2). Calcium is not easy to find by itself, but can be found in gypsum, dolomitic lime and some retail fertilizer blends like calcium nitrate. It may be available in organic versions like blood meal or bone meal. This will be discussed later.

Picture #2

Sulfur

Sulfur helps with chlorophyll and protein production. Usually, the parts of the country that get more rainfall are more acidic and have more of this naturally occurring then those that don't.

Magnesium

Magnesium is part of the chlorophyll in all healthy plants. It is readily available from magnesium sulfate, which is also known as Epsom salts and is commonly used in the greenhouse market as a fertilizer. Tomatoes, peppers, and potatoes like extra magnesium.

Picture #3

Iron

Iron helps nitrogen be more efficient. When the pH of the soil is high (above 6.5), naturally occurring iron will become tied up in the soil and unavailable (Picture #3). This can happen in areas where the alkalinity of the water source is high. No matter where you live, the addition of a little chelated iron on a regular basis is hardly ever a bad thing.

Silicon

A relatively new beneficial element has come onto the scene in recent years - silicon. This is not the same stuff you use to caulk your bathroom walls or the stuff used by doctors for breast augmentations. It is an element found in native soils, but has been absent in soil-less media. It is taken up into the plant and accumulates in cell walls, which strengthens the plant tissues. It creates stronger plants, stronger stems, and improved root mass. It also improves resistance to insects and disease and shows increased drought tolerance. Just the added drought tolerance alone, when growing in containers, is worth considering the addition of this important element to your soil mixes.

Other Micro Nutrients

Boron, manganese, zinc, copper, chloride, and molybdenum. I will not get into each of these and what they do. Just know plants can suffer if they do not have a well balanced diet. Think of all of the above nutrients as a big multivitamin that will help the plants general overall health and wellness. Most balanced fertilizers on the market today will have different ratios of all of the above nutrients, but it is always good to read the label.

Fertilizer Types

Basically, fertilizer comes in two types: synthetic (inorganic) or organic. In my 60 plus years of living I have learned there are a few things you just don't bring up in social conversations: politics, religion, sexual orientation, and organic vs. inorganic fertilizers. There are strong feelings one way or another and, in the case of organic vs. inorganic fertilizers, not a lot seems based upon science.

Remember my story in the overview? I grew up with a father who was a conventional gardener only to become an organic convert. Then after several years of struggle, he became more of a moderate; doing a combination of both organic and conventional. That is where I am today. So I am not going to try and talk you into one way or another. Do what feels right for you.

Synthetic Granular Fertilizer

Synthetic granular fertilizer comes in many different forms, but most of us are familiar with the types of fertilizers we apply to our lawns. This is generally a large prilled fertilizer that uses natural gas in its creation. Because it is synthetic in nature, nitrogen (the #1 nutrient) can be produced at a higher value than organic sources. For example, ammonium sulfate is 21-0-0. Urea is 46-0-0. Though this might sound tempting to use in our containers, these products contain too much nitrogen and release it very quickly. Unless you are careful, you will blow your plants out of the ground by either too much top growth or by actually burning and killing them. There are better options.

Coated Fertilizer

For containers, I recommend you use coated fertilizers. Yes, they are still synthetic in nature, but the coating will slow down the release of the fertilizer. This will measure out the fertilizer over time so that the potential for plant burn or over feeding is reduced. Many of these can be purchased by length of time release. For example, you can purchase fertilizers that will release over a 3 month, 6 month, 9 month, or even longer time period. One of the benefits of these types of fertilizers is if you are not good at fertilizing on a regular basis, these fertilizers can be blended into the soil at the beginning of the year and release slowly throughout the summer. Osmocote© and Dynamite© are two examples of a coated fertilizer.

Make sure to get a slow release fertilizer that will last long enough to cover all of your growing needs or plan on supplementing with other sources as you go through the season!

One thing to remember - since we can start planting *so* early it is very likely your 3 month slow release fertilizer will run out of nutrients sometime in May or June. Here's why: most coated fertilizers will slowly release based upon soil temperatures, with 70° F being the average mean temperature. Using the *Container Gardening in 3D* system, you will be warming your soils up into the 50-60° F range with the use of a SolarCap®. A 3 month fertilizer will last about 4 months - and that's being optimistic. So either purchase a longer release coated fertilizer (like 6-9 months), or be prepared to add more fertilizer during the summer months (like the water soluble fertilizers mentioned below). Otherwise, as the fertilizer begins to peter out, your plants will slowly starve causing them to decline before they reach the end of the growing season, resulting in a loss of yield.

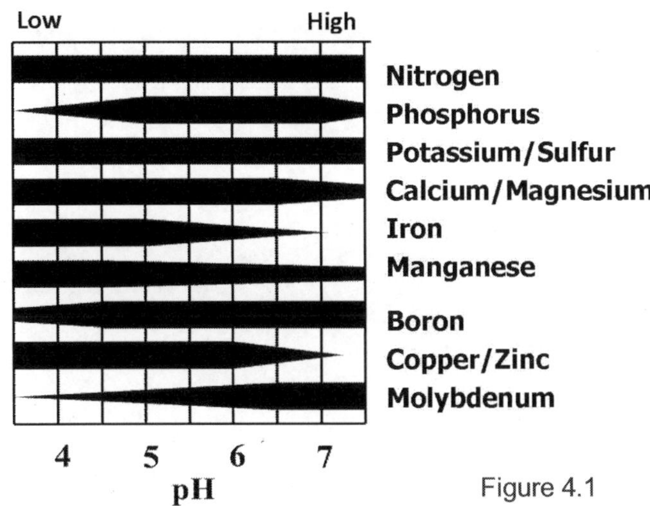

Figure 4.1

Water Soluble Synthetic Fertilizers

Water soluble synthetic fertilizers also work great in containers, but because of the way these fertilizers release, they need to be applied more often then the coated version. These usually take a teaspoon or two per gallon of water every week or so and contain more of the micro nutrients that may not be found in the coated versions. Also, if you are struggling with pH (see pH chart on the right, Figure 4.1), one can use soluble fertilizers to help change the pH of the soil in the container. This takes some effort, but is possible. Miracle-Gro© and Peters© are two examples of water soluble fertilizers.

A great way to have a successful container garden is to use both types of fertilizer. Blend in some coated fertilizer at the initial planting, then use the water soluble every 2-3 weeks throughout the year. As I mentioned above, it is hard to find a good source of calcium in a granular form, but if you hunt around, you can find it. There are also some water soluble fertilizers that will have it as part of the analysis. Some brands focusing on the needs of tomatoes may have a higher percentage of calcium.

Organic Granular Fertilizer

Organic granular fertilizers are typically *very* low in nitrogen. Because soil-less media (remember there is no dirt or garden soil in potting soil) contains virtually no fertilizer, the combination of the two can leave plants showing signs of nitrogen deficiency. You may have to fertilize with an organic liquid more often to keep the plants from yellowing. Just by their nature, most organic fertilizers release very slowly. That can be a really good or bad thing. If you want a slow even response, great. If you are looking for a bit of a kick-in-the-butt immediate impact, not so great. Usually a liquid version of an organic fertilizer will release quicker than the granular kind.

Most organic fertilizers will not burn. I say "most" because some are poorly made and can be high in salts. Synthetic fertilizer on the other hand can burn plants quite easily and push more top growth at the expense of fruit growth. Make sure you know rates and release times for *all* fertilizers you may be using.

Some organic fertilizer groupies are using an organic fertilizer because they are also trying to change the soil texture or structure. Just remember that you are wasting your time if that is your intent here. Not that it won't work. Given enough time and the right amendments this soil-less media will change as well, but in reality, it would take many years. *Since the peat moss will break down further than I like, I empty my containers at least every 3 years and start over with fresh potting soil anyway.* If you want to change the texture, then add compost, but again, be careful as not all composts are created equal. Some will have the potential to be so high in salts you will only see stunted growth.

Organic Soluble Fertilizer

Since the legalization of marijuana in many states, the options for liquid organic fertilizers have exploded. Many are way over priced, in my opinion, to meet the marijuana markets' specific demographics and are what I would consider as Foo Foo juice - a little fertilizer in a lot of water. Stick with something simple with a good performance record, like fish emulsion. Just realize that most fish fertilizers come with quite a strong odor, so I strongly recommend you *do not* do any mixing inside the house.

pH and How it Effects Nutrient Availability

As we discussed briefly in chapter 3, pH is the measure of acidity or alkalinity of the soil. What a lot of people don't understand is how pH can affect the amount of nutrients your plants can actually get from the soil or the fertilizer that you may be adding. Anything below the pH of 7 is

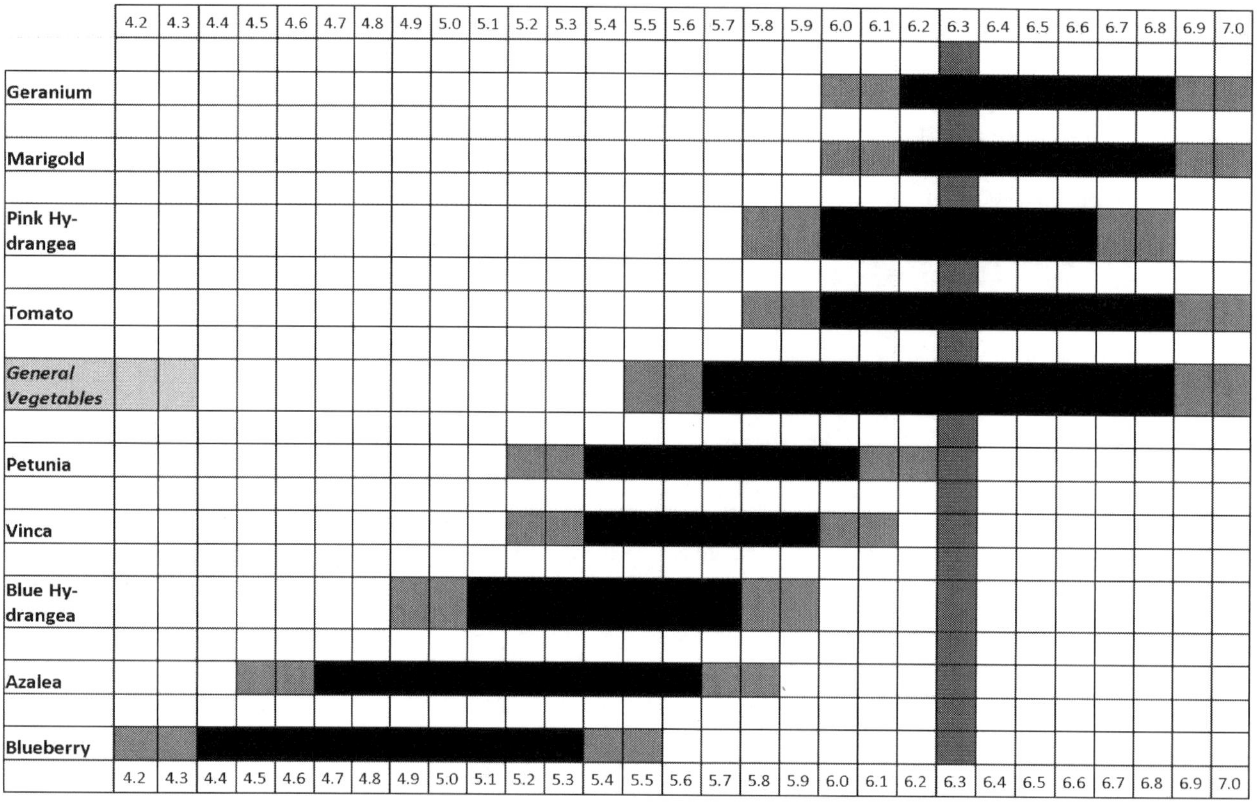

	4.2	4.3	4.4	4.5	4.6	4.7	4.8	4.9	5.0	5.1	5.2	5.3	5.4	5.5	5.6	5.7	5.8	5.9	6.0	6.1	6.2	6.3	6.4	6.5	6.6	6.7	6.8	6.9	7.0
Geranium																													
Marigold																													
Pink Hy-drangea																													
Tomato																													
General Vegetables																													
Petunia																													
Vinca																													
Blue Hy-drangea																													
Azalea																													
Blueberry																													
	4.2	4.3	4.4	4.5	4.6	4.7	4.8	4.9	5.0	5.1	5.2	5.3	5.4	5.5	5.6	5.7	5.8	5.9	6.0	6.1	6.2	6.3	6.4	6.5	6.6	6.7	6.8	6.9	7.0

Figure 4.2

considered acidic, and likewise, anything over the pH of 7 is considered to be basic. Refer back to the pH chart on page 41 (Figure 4.1). Notice how the availability of any nutrient, except nitrogen, is tied to the pH of the soil. This means that if you have really alkaline soil you may have problems with iron chlorosis, a yellowing effect on the plant. Likewise, a low pH will tend to tie up the nutrients of phosphorus and molybdenum.

The question is often asked, "Well, how can I tell if I live in an acidic pH area, or an alkaline one?" To gauge this, ask yourself some fairly easy questions. For example, do you have hard or soft water? Do you own a water conditioner? If you have hard water and need a water conditioner, then it's more than likely that the pH of your water is somewhere above 7 and that means it's alkaline. If your water is alkaline, it will change the pH of your soil over time, even it starts out being acidic.

You can also look around at the plants that grow in your area. Look at the pH Range of some general plants chart (Figure 4.2). Plants will naturally grow where it suits them best. Man sometimes tries to force plants to grow where they do not grow naturally because they can manipulate the environment, but sometimes these experiments fail. Think of those who try growing azaleas or blueberries in Utah. It doesn't work very well because Utah has alkaline soil and blueberries and azaleas like it quite acidic.

You can also use hydrangeas as a guide. As the chart shows, if the hydrangeas bloom is pink in your area, then your natural soil is going to be on the high side. If it flowers blue then it is acidic. Of course, if you get blue and pink blossoms on the same plant, then you are most likely in a fairly neutral area.

Fertilizer can also have an effect in soil-less media and can be used to adjust the pH if necessary. Is the pH getting too high? Add some Miracle-Gro© Acid fertilizer or something containing sulfur. If you need the opposite, to raise the pH, add some lime. Luckily for us most of our vegetables love to have the pH somewhere right in the middle. Notice the line going down from the pH range of 6.3. This is slightly acidic but you can see that this is a perfect range for many of the vegetables that we want to grow. Just remember that the pH can also be affected by the water, the environment, and even the plants themselves.

One more thought, look at Figure 4.2 again. As I've discussed, it is easy to see that some plants naturally favor different pH ranges. For example, look at the pH range for petunia's (5.4-6.1) compared to geraniums (6.2-6..8). The challenge comes when folks try to put drastically different pH loving plants, like these two, into the same container. Since it is so hard to keep a pH range right in the middle, this means some of the plants will be happy while others will not. When planting any container, try to put the same types of pH plants together. You will enjoy much more success.

It is important to have at least a vague idea of your area's pH as it will not only affect what nutrients are available, but also what plants you can grow.

"Knowing is not enough, we must apply ...

Being willing is not enough, we must do"

Leonardo da Vinci

Chapter 5

The How To...Let's Get Dirty!

Okay, time for the rubber to meet the road so to speak. This is where you learn the "how to" of creating a *Container Gardening 3D* container.

Items you will need:

1. Container of your choice.

2. Something to sit on - 5 gallon buckets or pails are perfect.

3. Three to four small plastic cups - plastic will last longer than wax paper.

4. Finger tool - the number one tool you will need to plant your containers is your index finger.

5. Seeds - have all the cool season veggie varieties you will need ready to go. We will be planting warm season plants later in the season (assuming you are doing this in the very early spring, of course).

6. Fertilizer - if you have some controlled release fertilizer (CRF), now is the time. Add about 1 lb. of CRF per 3 cubic foot bag of soil.

7. Bag(s) of pre-mixed potting soil (soil-less media).

8. Any other soil amendments or fertilizers you might be adding, i.e., zeolite, compost, silicon, etc.

Step #1

Picture #1

Get all of your materials together. Find something comfortable to sit on. I have an assortment of old 5 gallon buckets from my home remodeling days, but you can find 5 gallon buckets at any hardware store easy enough. Use anything that is comfortable for you. The point is you will not need to get down on your knees (Picture #1).

(If you do not have any controlled release fertilizer (CRF) or additional soil amendments to add, skip to step #2).

Pour approximately half of the potting soil into the container and add 1/4th of the CRF you have measured out. Add half of any additional soil amendment you may have as well.

Picture #2

This is the fun part!

With your hands mix all the materials into the soil. Try to get everything mixed as uniformly throughout the soil as you can.

Why mix only 1/4th of the fertilizer into 1/2 of the soil? Because not all of the roots will make it down to the bottom of the container, and nitrogen, being very mobile, will move through the soil and possibly leach out the bottom. Why waste it?

Add the remaining soil, CRF, or any soil amendments and blend till you get a uniform consistency (Picture #2).

Step #2

(If you are skipping Step #1, start here). Add the soil to the brim of the container. Wiggle the container back and forth a bit and see how much it settles. DO NOT pack the soil down. Once

If you forget Step #1, you can still add the CRF or other fertilizer on top of the soil once it is planted, but it won't be as effective! But not soil amendments.

Figure 5.1 Planting Chart

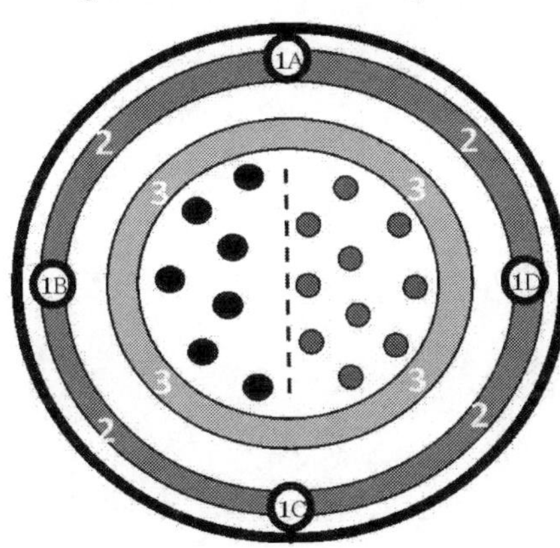

wiggled, see if you need to add any additional soil to bring the soil level up to about one inch below the brim. If you are there already, perfect! As you work with the container the soil will settle even more. Do not pack the soil with your hands as that will only take away valuable air space.

You are now ready to start planting!

Make a cross in the soil like points on a compass: east, west, north, south. This helps to know where to position the small plastic cups, which are meant to hold the place of larger plants you will incorporate later, i.e. tomatoes, peppers, cucumbers, etc. Look at the planting chart above (Figure 5.1, which, weirdly enough, is kind of beginning to look like a pizza!). These place holder cups represent numbers 1A-1D or 1A-1C, depending on your chosen configuration of either 4 Zone 1 plants or only 3 (See Zone 1, page 13). For our purposes here, we will be planting 4 plants.

Make sure to turn the cups upside down so that they do not collect water, which could become a hosting ground for insects like mosquitoes. See Picture #3.

Step #3

Take your plastic cups and place them *upside down* towards the end of the cross section lines (Picture #3). You can experiment with placing them as close to the edge of the pot as possible or moving them in a couple of inches. I have found that in the larger containers (30 inch diameter), I can afford to move them in a little from the edge. On the smaller ones (21 inch diameter), I need the room, so I move them out to the very edge. Both options work well. As long as the cups end up on the *outside* of where you will be placing your tomato cages, you will be okay.

Picture #3

Take your gardening tool (index finger) and make a shallow trough completely around the pot about 1½ - 2 inches from the edge. This gives you the guide for your first row of veggies (See Figure 5.1). This is where your planning will come in handy. Here you can plant carrots, radishes, or other cool season vegetables (Picture #3).

For carrots it is imperative to make the trough very shallow and clean out any big debris that might remain in there, such as pieces of bark or clumps of peat. Because carrot seeds are so small, planting them too deeply will only lead to frustration and sorrow, as they will not germinate successfully. On the other hand, that is one of the benefits of using a soil-less media. It is very light, which makes it easier to germinate seeds than regular garden soil. But I digress, back to the planting!

Step #4

Picture #4

If you are planting carrots, take a pinch of seeds between your forefinger and thumb and just like adding sprinkles of pepper or salt to a recipe, sprinkle the seeds around the trough (Picture #4). Remember: how far you go around depends on how many veggies you want to harvest at any one time. Do you want to harvest them all at the same time or do you want to spread them out? Usually for a 21 inch pot, I plant the whole row. For bigger seeds, like radishes, plant them about every 1 inch apart. I use my planting tool (index finger) and make little indentations in the soil about 1/2 inch deep around the circle I just made. Put one to two radish seeds per hole. Do not cover seeds at this time!

Picture #5

Step #5

Inside the first trough, make another shallow trench about 2 inches away (Figure 5.1). If I planted carrots in the first row, this one may be radishes or visa versa (Picture #5).

Do not cover the seeds with soil at this time! You will do this later when you are all done planting.

Picture #6

Step #6

Go back to your north-south line that cut your pot in half. With your finger tool, make 3/4 inch indentations about every 2-3 inches apart in a triangular fashion on one side of the line. Here you can plant lettuce, spinach or any other Level 1 cool season vegetable (black dots on left, Figure 5.1, Picture #6).

Step #7

Now do the same thing on the other side of the line. You can plant the same thing on this side as well, but I usually plant another cool season vegetable, such as spinach, swiss chard, lettuce, etc. (dots on right, Figure 5.1, Picture #6).

Picture #7

Step #8

Use your hand and smooth the soil over all of the holes and trenches you've made. I typically use the back of my hand because I feel I can backfill the holes easier this way without pressing down too hard, which will end up packing the soil (Picture #7).

<u>DO NOT PACK DOWN THE SOIL!!!</u> Remember, packing the soil may affect the germination percentage in a bad way, as it only makes it harder for some of the seeds to germinate and reach the top of the soil. Carrots are especially susceptible to this so resist the urge. If watered correctly, the soil will pack its self down!

Step #9

Picture #8

Time to water. Make *sure* you have a water breaker nozzle of some kind to water this in (Picture #8). *Do not* use a direct stream of water as it will either dig a huge hole or at the very least, disrupt the soil and disturb the seed bed. Take a look at Picture #9 on the next page. Notice the big hole? I asked a friend to water while I was out of town and came home to find this.

Picture #9

Obviously, a water breaker nozzle was not used (I thought for sure I left one on the end of that hose … *still* trying to figure out where it went). As a result, all of the tiny seeds placed in a very shallow trench were displaced and plants came up in a haphazard mess. A water breaker nozzle, correctly used, will keep this from happening. Since most seeds are planted quite shallow, you do not need to water too deeply at this point, just make sure to water evenly all the way across the container.

Step #10

If your container garden is planted in the very early spring, now is the time to use a Solar-Cap®. It will warm the soil and provide adequate protection for the young plants during the stormy spring weather. I have planted these containers in January through February and had radishes up in 2 - 3 weeks. The other cool season plants will germinate and grow as the soil temperatures allow, but definitely earlier than if planted out in the cold garden soil. In fact, I am usually eating radishes before most folks even make it out to begin working their garden soil in the spring.

SOLARCap

Note!

Watering *- Just a note about watering the container after planting. In the very early spring, you will* not *need to water very often, if at all. However, you need to monitor the container, especially if you are using a season extender like a SolarCap®. The SolarCap® will heat up the soil and dry it out quicker than if exposed to the elements. Young seedlings are most susceptible when the seedling sends out it's first little root. If the soil dries during this critical time, it will kill the plant, so be very careful. If the only source of water you have in the early spring is snow, then just throw a little inside the SolarCap® and the sun will melt it.*

Note!

SolarCaps® are available at your nearest local independent garden center, farm supply store or at containicus.com

MCH Container Progression in Pictures

"When the well is dry, we know the worth of water"

Benjamin Franklin

Photo taken by Anton Cross

Chapter 6

Watering

There is much current debate about global warming or climate change and its affect on water availability. I don't care what you call it or even if you believe it or not, but there are parts of the country where water is the most precious resource. One does not have to go very far back in our history to find people who died defending their water rights or feuds that started over water that are still going on to this day. I have been watching trends and I feel that anything I can do to reduce my water consumption, the better.

So how does that apply to container gardening? I have done my share of watering in many different ways. I will share some thoughts about each.

Flood Irrigation

Back in the day when there were no pumps, pioneers built canals and channeled the water down furrows. This method of irrigation is still used today. Flood irrigation works quite well, as the water is run down furrows and soaks in right at the roots. Not much water is lost to evaporation and it does not involve getting the foliage of the plants wet. The challenge with flood irrigation is that you need to get the water to the "end of the row." It can take enormous amounts of water to get enough water to the end of the row; hence, the plants near the head gate get overwatered, so the plants at the end can get even just a little. Although you could set up a system with pots in a low trench and let water run down through them, this system is not practical for container usage.

Impact Sprinklers

Many folks water their gardens with impact sprinklers. You know, those kind that shoot out a straight stream of water that hits the revolving arm which in turn helps the head to move in a circle.

Impact head sprinklers typically cover many square feet at a time, sometimes shooting out to over 20 feet in distance. These are great when it is necessary to cover big areas at one time. The challenge with impact heads is that they need to be left on for long periods of time to be effective, and of necessity, get the tops of the plants wet as well. This can add to disease. Impact heads often overshoot areas immediately next to the sprinkler head in order to cover big spaces, so that areas right next to the head do not get as much water as at the end of the stream and because the water is shooting up into the air, it is susceptible to evaporation. It would be possible to set up an overhead system to water all of your containers at once. This is exactly what folks who have large field nurseries do, but for our containers, this system of watering is not practical either.

Hand Watering

In theory, hand watering is one of the most effective ways to water. If done correctly, only the plants that need watering will get it. The one doing the watering has complete control. Sounds perfect! Well, hang on there. There are two other things to consider: 1) How much is your time worth; and 2) what happens when you are not around? Many greenhouse owners know that if they leave the watering to untrained individuals in their absence, it can be a virtual train wreck by the time they get back. In fact, I have walked into many large greenhouse growing operations only to find the owner holding the end of a hose watering his plants. I usually can't resist making a snide remark about how they were reduced to doing what most people would consider a minimum waged job, but before the owner responded, I knew what the answer would be … "Watering is the most important job in the greenhouse." I knew the answer because I had heard it many times before and have observed the results of both good and bad hand watering.

Drip Irrigation

Basically drip irrigation is the process of using special emitters to slowly drip water into the container over a longer period of time, which allows the water to seep throughout the entire profile without you having to stand there watching. Chances are the watering will be more consistent and uniform, so less water will be leeching or running out the bottom of the container going to waste. If you end up with quite a few containers like I do, this is definitely a time saver.

Self Watering Container

Way back in Chapter 2 we mentioned self watering containers. Do they work? Yes, but they can also be quite expensive. For the size of pots that I like to grow in, we are talking in the $200-$300 range. If you have that kind of cash burning a hole in your pocket, then commercial self watering containers are a great way to go.

How you water is critical to success!

Since most folks will either hand water, drip irrigate, or use self watering containers I will discuss each of these in more detail.

Hand watering

For most individuals, hand watering is a totally acceptable way to water your containers, however, there are some important things to remember:

Picture #1

1) I strongly recommend using some kind of water breaker nozzle. This will keep the pressure of the water coming out of the hose from digging into and eroding the soil (Picture #1).

2) When you water, water through the ENTIRE soil profile. What do I mean by this? I think most folks have been trained to water till they see water coming out of the holes located on the bottom of the container, but what they usually miss is that when soil-less media dries out, it will shrink. This causes the soil to pull away from the edge of the container, which creates a great channel for water to run down, then out (Picture #2). If you are not careful you end up with a container with wet soil a few inches deep on the top, a few inches deep on the sides, and nothing wet in the very center (Figure 6.1, C). When hand watering it is important to water deeply and thoroughly so that the entire soil profile throughout the whole container gets wet, Figure 6.1, D). Failing to do so will create a situation where you may need to water multiple times a day to avoid wilting of plants during the heat of summer. Doing it properly means not having to water as often.

Picture #2

3) Next it is VERY important to let your soil dry out between watering's. Remember the graph shown in Chapter 3 (page 24), on the importance of air in the soil profile? None of the plants we choose to enjoy as veggies in our containers are bog plants. They must have some drying down time and allow air to permeate through the soil profile.

Figure 6.1. A. Soil fills the whole container. **B.** As it dries out, the soil begins to shrink, pulling away from the edge of the pot. **C.** Water will go where there is least resistance—down the sides and out. **D.** To properly water the container, the whole profile needs to receive moisture. It may mean watering the container several times, allowing the water a few moments to soak in between each watering.

That is why it is so imperative to water correctly in the first place. By wetting the entire profile at the same time consistently, the soil will dry down at about the same rate and the plant will get both the air and water that it needs to survive. Over watering brings unwanted diseases and insects.

It has been my experience that most people struggle with watering correctly; they either water everyday whether it needs it or not or not evenly enough to get the water through the entire profile. If you struggle to get it right at first, take heart! I see many professional greenhouse growers who suffer from the same problems. Correct watering can be learned and mastered.

4) Pay attention to the plants. Don't water them if they don't look like they need it. If they begin to wilt, give them a good, deep watering. You will notice at different times of the year and at different times of the life cycle of the plants, they will require different amounts of water. Earlier in the year, you may go several days between watering's and during the hot summer months you may need to water daily.

5) The location of the containers will make a difference as well. Are they up against a house where heat can be reflected or are they where they get some afternoon shade? Do you live in an area with high humidity or out in high desert areas? These will all make a difference on how fast they will dry out.

Drip Irrigation

One way to solve the challenges that are inherent with hand watering is to set your containers up on a drip irrigation system. They are fairly easy to do but beyond the scope of this book. Check your local irrigation supply stores or look online to get ideas.

Some of the advantages of drip irrigation are:

- Less time required compared to hand watering
- Fertilizer and nutrient loss is minimized due to localized application and reduced leaching
- Water application efficiency is high
- Moisture within the root zone can be more easily maintained
- Water distribution is highly uniform, controlled by output of each nozzle or drip hose
- Variation in supply can be regulated by regulating the valves and drippers
- Foliage remains dry, reducing the risk of disease
- Many containers can be irrigated all at the same time if set up in a series of emitters

The disadvantages of drip irrigation are:

- Expense: initial cost can be high
- Clogging: if the water is not properly filtered and the equipment not properly maintained, it can result in clogging
- Germination problems: in soil-less media drip systems may be unable to wet the soil surface for proper germination. This can be solved by hand watering until the seeds germinate and have good root systems before going to drip irrigation.

With drip irrigation, the same two problems can exist that are mentioned above:

1) There is too much water. Drips are great, but if the weather cools and the drip system is going on for three hours every day automatically, you will create a water logged bog. Plants will rot.

2) If some of your emitters become plugged, you will have some plants getting enough water, and some not at all. When you see some plants wilting, the natural thought is to increase the drip time. This obviously will not help. Check all of your emitters on a regular basis to make sure they are working properly.

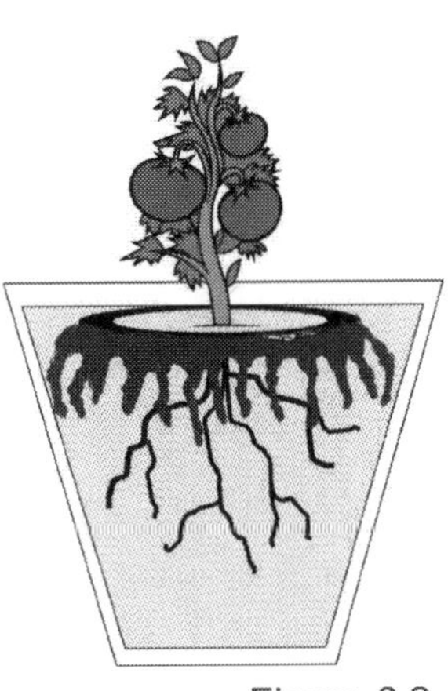

Figure 6.2

Although drip irrigation is a great way to go, don't get lazy. Be there often to check on how things are going. Challenges can come if you put your watering system on an automatic timer and expect bounteous harvests without checking on it ever again.

There are new drip irrigation products on the market that I use for my larger containers. These are meant for tree rings but fit perfectly inside my 30 inch containers, and because they hook up to a typical garden hose, I can set them up in a series. The picture below is a 5 foot Dramm© Tree Soaker Ring, 5/8 inch diameter. Make sure you reduce your water pressure by only opening your faucet slightly; the ring works best when used over a long period of time at low pressure and low flow. Water will slowly seep through the container till it is all saturated, (Figure 6.2). Higher pressures may blow bigger holes in the ring causing water to shoot up and out of the container. Not good.

Picture #3

Self Watering Container

The current rave of gardening on the internet, it seems, is how to make self watering containers out of 5 gallon buckets. There are some really good ideas out there, but as I have noted before my challenge is 5 gallon buckets are not big enough for me; I like to use containers that are bigger so as to get as much yield as possible out of every container. To that end, I have been working on creating my own self watering containers that are big enough to also work with SolarCaps®. I share this idea with you with the belief that self watering containers has the potential to be the future of water conservation as far as container gardening is concerned.

Take a look at Figure 6.3 to get the overall vision of what you will be creating, and please read through all directions to get the idea of HOW, before you start to DO. This will save you some time and money.

Self Watering Container Instructions

Items you will need:

1 - A 21 inch diameter, heavy duty bucket/container with NO drainage holes. (A)

1 - Wick basket (B)

1 - Dividing layer (C)

1 - 1½ inch plastic pipe length cut to fit; PVC or poly flex (D)

1 - 3/4 inch slip X 1/2 inch female threaded bushing (E)

1 - 1/2 inch male plug

1 - Cable strap, plastic 10 inch

Eco sealant or silicone caulk

Tools - Exacto knife or scissors

Drill with 1 & 3/8th inch bits

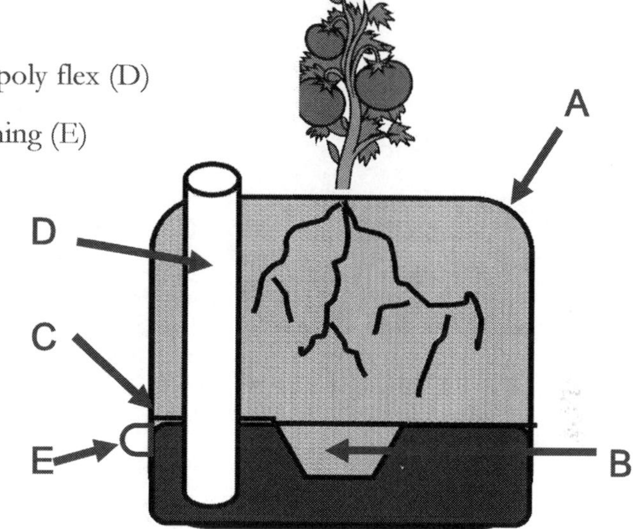

Figure 6.3

Step #1

Find the right container (A). You want one that *will not* have any holes in the bottom. The idea is to keep a reservoir of water inside the container. Make sure they will be durable enough to last several years, as you do not want to do this annually. I have found a product from Tuff Stuff® that are commonly referred to as muck buckets. These heavy duty buckets have no drain holes and the 21 inch diameter I am looking for (the 21 inch diameter will fit the SolarCaps®). You can find them or others like them at most local farm stores or on the internet. If they have rope handles, you can either leave them on to help move the containers around or cut them off. I leave them on (Picture #4).

Picture #4

Step #2

You will need to find a wick basket (B). This is meant to be filled with soil and will extend down into the water reservoir, which will

Your container CANNOT have any holes in the bottom!

then work to wick the water up to the top of the container. I have looked around and found several kitchen colanders that can work quite well. You can use other items for the same purpose, but here are a couple of things to look for. No matter what I choose, I don't want the holes so big that soil will escape through them, and if at all possible, it needs to have legs so it does not sit flat on the bottom of the container, as water needs to be able to get under the wick basket as well (Picture #5).

Picture #5

Step #3

A dividing layer (C) is necessary to keep the soil separated from the water reservoir. It will need to be water proof and sturdy enough that it will not collapse under the weight of the soil when it is wet. Soil-less media is very light weight when dry, but adding water will increase its bulk density many times over, and it can become quite heavy. Water weighs 8 lbs. per gallon so even if the soil is only holding two gallons of water in the soil, that is an additional 16 lbs. bearing down on your divider. So make sure it can handle the weight. For these containers, I used a 3 mil coroplast polypropylene product (Picture #6) that is often called "plastic cardboard". It worked, but was barely sturdy enough to handle the weight of the wet soil. If you go this route, find a thicker mil or double the coroplast.

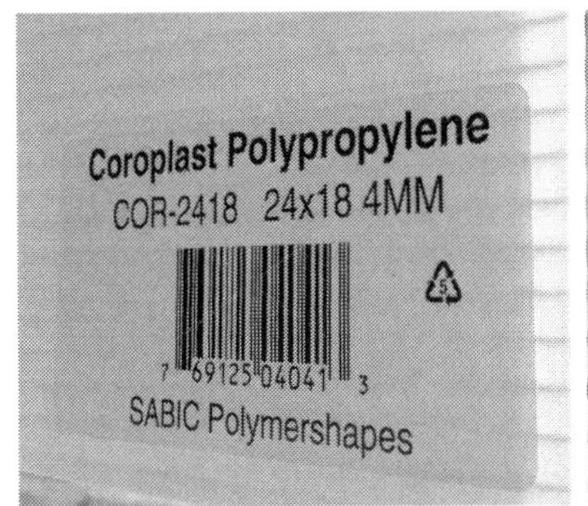

Picture #6

Cut the divider into a circle that will fit down into the pot and rest on top of the wick basket. This needs to be snug on the sides, but rest on top of the wick basket without any buckling of the divider. It may take a little trimming to get it right. If you are using the same 21 inch muck bucket, the diameter of the circle will be AROUND 17 inches. (Diameter size can change due to size and shape of wick basket chosen). Place the wick basket on the bottom of the container and measure across to get the real diameter (Picture #7).

Picture #7

Cut the dividing layer to fit TIGHT into the container. This will help hold it up when the soil is added.

Step #4

Cut a hole out of the center of the divider smaller than the top of the wick basket. The support the wick basket can give to the divider is so important the hole in the divider can be a couple of inches less than the width of the colander/wick basket and still work quite well (Picture #8).

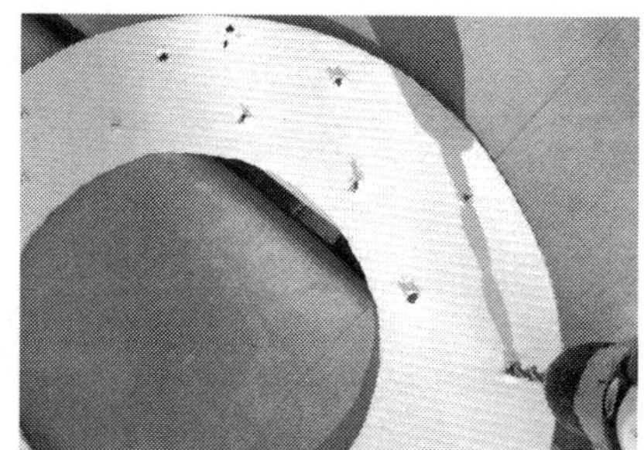

Picture #8

Step #5

Drill 3/8th inch holes randomly in the divider. There needs to be enough holes to allow water to pass through the divider into the reservoir, but not so many that it looks like shredded cheese and compromises the dividers strength (Picture #8).

Step #6

Cut your 1½ inch poly pipe (D) to be about 6-8 inches above the lip of your container. This will be inserted down into the reservoir, through the divider and will be a source of adding water and nutrients. I bevel out one end of the pipe so nothing can block the opening as it needs to allow water to flow freely into the reservoir (Picture #9).

Picture #9

Step #7

Cut a hole in the divider to allow the pipe to go down into the reservoir (Picture #10). *Optional:* When the soil is placed into the container, the pipe should be held in place, but you can attach pipe to the side of the container with cable ties. Make sure to leave enough slack for the pipe to go down through (Picture #11).

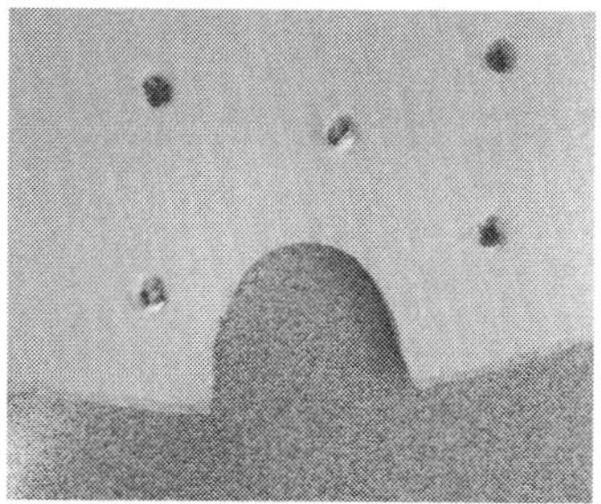

Picture #10

Picture #11

Picture #12

Step #8

Drill a 1 inch drain hole on side of the container just *below* the height of the dividing layer. With no drainage holes in the bottom the possibility exists that we could overfill our containers and thus drown the plants. This allows water to over flow out of the container, and the ability to freshen up the water when necessary. You may need to ream this out a bit to get the 3/4" x 1/2" plastic bushing to fit into the hole (Picture #12).

Step #9

Glue the 3/4" x 1/2" plastic bushing (E) into the hole. I use eco friendly adhesive (Eco Bond© Farm Safe Adhesive), but you can use what ever glue or caulk that suits your fancy. Add a 1/2 inch plug (Picture #13).

Picture #13

Step #10

Put a light layer of adhesive on top of wick basket, or use cable ties and attach the divider ring. This will keep the wick basket from shifting if you end up moving the container. Make sure the divider is centered and will go down easily into the container before cementing in place. Put the pipe down through the divider. The finished product should look something like what you see below (Picture #14).

You are now ready to add soil!

Adding soil

Some say you need to pack the soil into the wick basket, but I don't agree. Add in the soil like you normally would. Fill the container up half way, add some slow release, shake the container a little to help settle the soil, fill it up to an inch from the top with more soil, add more slow release, shake a bit more, and you are done. As for the soil itself, I like something with coco fiber in it to help with the wicking action.

Picture #14

Watering

When the container is young, all watering should be over the top to keep the seedlings moist. Filling the reservoir is not necessary at this point in time. Once the weather begins to warm however, you have a choice: you can either continue watering over the top or use the tube to keep the reservoir filled. An advantage of watering over the top is the entire soil profile becomes saturated and the extra water will filter down into the reservoir, thereby adding to the days between watering.

One way to know if the reservoir is full is to let water weep out the drain hole. Due to the possibility of salt build up (and if you are not doing so already) it is recommended to water down through the top once a month or so to flush salts back down into the reservoir. I tend to keep the plug out all summer when I am home and watch the plants to know when I need to add more water. Some plants, like peppers, will appreciate the chance to dry out a bit. If you wish, you can make a plumb bob or dip stick to insert into the tube to ascertain the depth of the water in the reservoir.

Right before I leave for any extended period, I water over the top until the water comes out of the drain hole in the bottom. I then insert the plug and add a little bit more water. This will give me a few extra days worth of water in the reservoir.

Remember: leaving the plug in <u>all of the time</u> may lead to a prolonged saturation of water in the soil profile, resulting in less air space and the very real possibility of death to plants. <u>Always</u> keep in mind the ratio between soil, air, and water! (See Figure 3.3, page 26)

When using self watering containers, always keep in mind the ratio between, soil, air and water!

Q & A

I can't find a colander that will work…is there anything else I can use for a wick basket?

The great thing about colanders is they have a built in system of drainage holes. But yes, I have tried other things as well, i.e. plastic bowls, plastic hanging baskets, etc., anything I can get that is about 10-12 inches across and is about 4-5 inches deep. The deeper the wick basket the more potential water holding the reservoir will be, but don't go crazy. There still needs to be enough soil depth to support the root demand. Of course, since some of these did not come with pre-made holes like a colander, I had to drill holes all over the place to allow water to flow easily in and out of the wick basket. Use a small enough drill bit so soil will not fall out of the holes easily.

Does it matter if I use PVC pipe instead of Poly Flex for the water tube (D)?

Only you can answer that question. Some fear that the PVC will degrade over time and will release poly chlorides into the soil environment and others frankly don't care. The PVC that is exposed to the sun will definitely get more brittle than the Poly Flex pipe. If you are concerned about either of these two issues then use the Poly Flex pipe that is approved for cold water in all new houses. Sometimes you can find precut pieces at hardware stores. But really, the way these self watering systems are built, when it becomes necessary, replacing the feeder tube is quite simple.

How do I know when to add more water to the reservoir?

Ahh, this is where the "rubber meets the road" so to speak with these containers. There are several ways you can do this. As already mentioned, one is to create a dip stick that you can measure how much water is in the reservoir. Fill the reservoir till water comes out the drain hole. Put the dip stick down the tube and mark the water level on the stick. This is your base mark showing the reservoir completely full. You can gauge when to add more water when you notice the water way down on the dip stick.

The other way is to just watch your plants. If they begin to wilt, the reservoir is obviously empty and it's time to refill! The good thing about this method is that it's not a bad thing to let the soil dry down once in a while.

Actually, the very best method is to use a combination of both of these. If you use a dip stick you will be aware when you are getting low on water. This way you will be ready for the beginning signs of wilt, instead of being surprised by it, thus you can prevent wilting before it gets to a point that is damaging while you are away.

Notes

"Plant carrots in January and you'll never have to eat carrots"

Author Unknown

Chapter 7

Peripherals

I just had to include the quote on the left even though I respectfully disagree with the Unknown Author. Why? Because for over the past four years I have been planting carrots in January and enjoying great success.

So far, we have talked about the importance of using the right container, soil, fertilizer, and water nozzles. In this chapter, we will discuss several other components that will be just as important to your *Container Gardening in 3D* success. They really can be the difference maker in my 3D system and one of the main reasons I have such great success with those carrots that were planted in January. Let's get to it.

Season Extenders

One of the key components of the *Container Gardening in 3D* system is to use what I call season extenders. The idea after all, is to get the maximum yield out of each container. To do this, one needs to start as early as possible and keep the plants going for as late as possible. There are several products on the market that help with this and I would like to take the time to talk about some of them.

Early Spring

Cloches

If you looked up the word 'cloche' in the dictionary, you would find something like this: "A bell-shaped glass-cover placed over a plant to protect it from frost and to force its growth." Cloches have been used for centuries in countries like France and were originally made of glass. Placing individual glass bell jars over each and every plant has grown out of favor in our modern day agriculture, but shadows still exist. Today cloches are made of light weight synthetic fabric and are usually placed

Picture #1

directly on low hoops covering entire rows of plants, which is much more economical and feasible than individual glass covers.

In the home market, you may recognize cloches by products like Hot Kaps© or Wall-O-Waters©. They protect young plants from early frost, hail, snow, high winds or whatever the unpredictable spring weather can throw at them. Hot Kaps© and Wall-O-Waters© work a little bit differently from one another.

Hot Kaps© (Picture #1) are a self supporting cover that allows the plants to grow up protected till they come out of the top. It is meant to be removed once the threat of frost is gone. It is very easy to use and quite idiot proof. Not a lot can go wrong using this product. Some use upside down plastic milk jugs to accomplish the same purpose.

One needs to be careful not to leave milk jugs in place too long. A hot spring day will basically cook anything that is beneath it.

Picture # 2

Wall-O-Waters© (or others of the same ilk, Picture #2), on the other hand are individual tubes that require them to be filled with water to help the product stand erect. These individual water tubes then form a teepee of water that allows the sun to heat up the cold garden soil to increase growth early in the spring. They work great unless one of the tubes happens to spring a leak, which causes the whole teepee to lean. If enough water is lost, the whole Wall-O-Water© can fall over. Consequently, you will also see mending kits for sale along with these products. The other challenge I find with these products is deciding when to take them off. They work so well and the plants come out of the top so fast that you fear taking them off too early. However, if you wait too long then they are hard to get off as the plant has grown out of the top. I have found that some plants have no stem strength and tend to fall over if these are left on too long, so timing is everything with these. Having said that, for the typical home gardener growing out in regular garden soil, I am a big believer in Hot Kaps© and Wall-O-Waters©. The problem is they do not work for my 3D system.

SolarCap®

One of the challenges of both products above is that they can only cover one plant at a time and as we have already discussed, the *Maximus Containicus Horticus* motto means I am trying to get as ***much*** as I can out of ***every*** container. One cover per plant was not working for me. I wanted to have something that would allow me to cover the ENTIRE container so I could get a jump on planting the whole container, not just specific plants. So I began to look around. Nothing I saw did what I was

hoping to do so I invented my own: SolarCap®. It is one of the key components of *Container Gardening in 3D*.

All cloches are meant to harness the energy of the sun and warm up the soil during the early time of the year. Like sitting in your car on a clear, but cold day, you can feel the warmth of the sun coming through the windshield. Indeed, the car can warm up to temperatures much warmer than the cold outside air. In a sense they become mini greenhouses.

SOLARCap

A SolarCap® is meant to do the same thing, *but does it over the* ***entire*** *container*, not individual plants. I have run tests during the early spring and air temperatures inside the SolarCap® can be 10-20° warmer than the outside air. Because the air is warming the soil, the soil temperatures warm up enough to germinate cool season veggies like radishes, lettuce, spinach, and carrots.

Picture #3

As an experiment, I planted radishes, lettuce, spinach, and carrots in January. I put on my SolarCap® and placed the pot next to the southern exposure of my brick home. I kept two different thermometers: one inside the SolarCap® and one attached to my garage not far away. After several days, I checked both thermometers and it was basically 35° warmer inside the SolarCap® (Picture #3). I kept track throughout the spring, and during the day, it was always at least 20° warmer inside the SolarCap®.

Picture #4

I also had a soil thermometer placed in the soil. After several days with the SolarCap® on this is what I saw (Picture #4). A soil temperature of 40°. Remember, this was during January in Utah. I had to *unfreeze* the soil before I could even get it into the container.

Picture #5

Here is the same thermometer a 3 weeks later (Picture #5). Notice the small plants near by? These are the seeds germinating - in February!

Finally, look at Picture #6. This is a month later. Since all cool season plants will only germinate after the soil temperature reaches around 40° F, the only thing stopping you from enjoying earlier crops is how fast you can warm up the soil. With the SolarCap®, I have found I can grow cool season crops almost anytime of the year. Warm season veggies are much more particular about outside air temperatures, but hey, I will take what I can get without paying natural gas prices to heat up a large greenhouse.

Picture #6

Because of where I located this container, I had no access to water unless I hauled it out by hand. I was pondering the problem when I realized I had water all around me…snow! When the soil began to dry out, I simply took a small shovel full of snow and dropped it into the top of the Solar-Cap®. In two days, all of the snow had melted, thus it did the watering for me. (See the progression pictures, Picture #7). Even though the air temperature outside was still in the 30's, you can see that the air temperature during the day warmed up quite nicely, and the soil temperature was consistently above 40 degrees. One caveat; this may not work if the plants are just emerging and the air temperature is below 20° F, as it may freeze tender young plants. Wait for air temperatures to warm up above 30° F.

I also employ SolarCaps® after planting my warm season veggies later in the season so as to give them a head start. Though they will not protect warm season plants from hard frosts, they will keep the plants protected from many of the wild swings early spring weather can experience, such as hail, snow, high winds, etc. I have had these covers on during winds over 50 mph without losing them and thereby protecting the plants. Because they warm the soil, the warm season plants do not have to be placed in cold garden soil temperatures, thus eliminating some of the transplant shock all plants go through. They are also big enough to allow the plants room to grow and there will not be any plant damage when you decide to take them off.

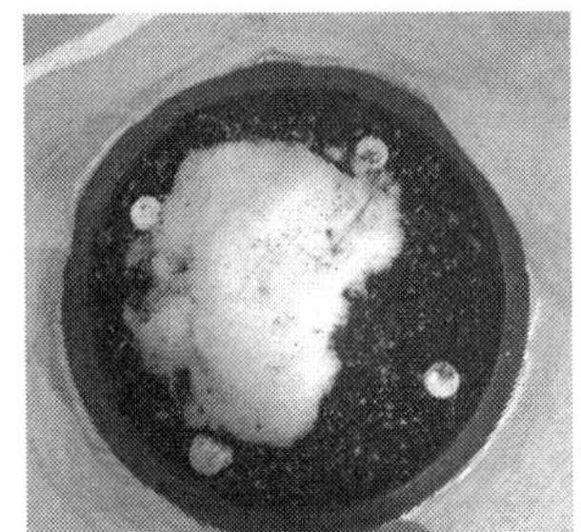

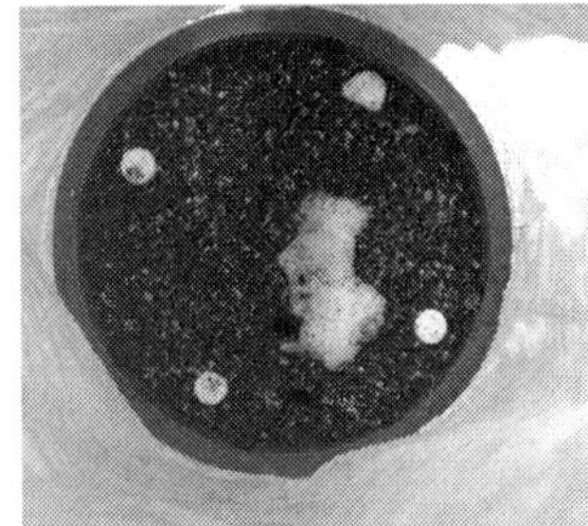

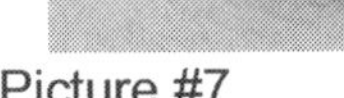

Picture #7

Summer

During the summer months, it is usually so hot *any* cover you put on plants will only cause burning of leaf tissue. Even the most warm season plants can experience leaf scorch. For that reason, covers are not even thought of during these months.

If you are going to plant late summer for fall crops while the temperatures are still pretty warm, you can use a SolarCap® to cover the containers to help them germinate quicker and get a faster start. You will definitely need to keep up on the watering as the Caps will cause the soil to dry out that much quicker. This will take some experimentation.

Fall

Picture #8

In the Fall, one can extend the season of harvest by covering the containers with either blankets or frost cloths (Picture #8). This will help with light frosts, but for heavy freezes take the pots inside or just decide the season is over. Or you can have even more fun by planting more containers!

Fall/Winter Crops

Obviously we would all like to eat fresh tomatoes, peppers, cucumbers, and the like out of the garden all year long. Mother Nature has other plans, and to a point, we have to acquiesce to her wishes. Still there are really lots of cool season veggies that we can enjoy. If you have reached your fill of gardening and are ready to put it all away in favor of football season, stop reading now. You have had a great summer season. Enjoy it and take a break. See you next spring. For those of you who cannot get enough of growing your own veggies: keep reading.

The first thing to know is, yes, it's possible to push the growing season later into the fall, early winter, and depending on where you live, through the winter months.

If you are interested, then I would get the *Fall & Winter Gardening Catalog* from Territorial Seed Company. Territorial Seed is located in Cottage Grove, Oregon. I have been reading their catalogs for years and respect the research that goes into their seed collections. They have great charts, advice, and recommendations. You can reach them at 541-942-9547, 8-5 Pacific Time Zone.

Just remember that the SolarCap® can be your best friend. Anything you start in your containers can be germinated quicker, grown to maturity faster, and protected under the SolarCap®. I have had carrots go through the whole winter and were still fresh the next spring. My sister did the same with spinach.

Experiment!

Plant Supports

As we discussed in chapter 1 (The Concept, page 11), *Container Gardening in 3D* means we are taking advantage of all the space allotted to us. This definitely includes the space above the container. To do this successfully, we will need some supports, which are also known as cages or trellises.

If you are a fan of *WWF Wrestle Mania: Steel Cage Challenge*, "The Cage" will mean something entirely different for you than what we are talking about here, but the cage is a very important part of Maximus Containicus Horticus or getting the most out of your container garden. Most folks will know these as they are more commonly known: tomato cages. Indeed, we will be using them to help with our tomatoes, but they can be used for so much more than that! Let's take some time to look at the different ways these cages can be used and the criteria I use to select them. Criteria first.

I look for cages that are strong enough not to fall over. We have all probably seen or experienced cages that cannot stand the weight of the plants when they begin fruiting and end up on the ground. Useless!

Here are the three main things I look for in a cage:

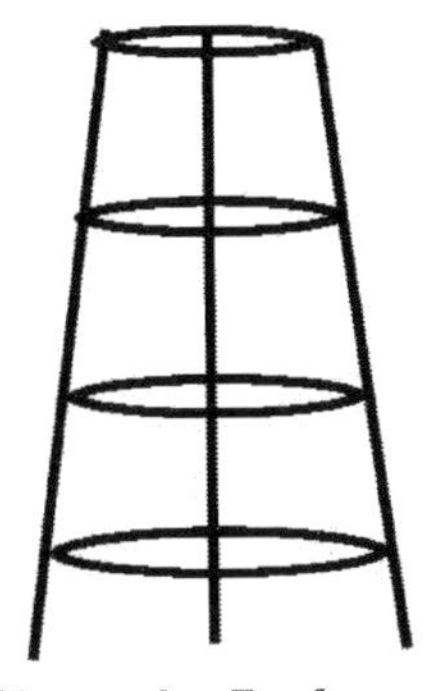

Shape A - Preferred

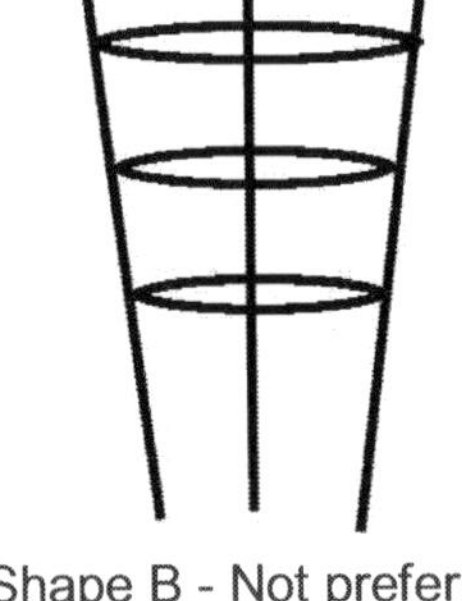

Shape B - Not preferred

The shape - I want it to look more like an old Mayan temple than a snow cone (see right). I have **never** had Shape A fall over, while the same cannot be said for Shape B.

The gauge of wire - It makes sense that the smaller the gauge of wire, the weaker the cage will be. Look for cages with heavier gauged wire.

The coating - Many cages are made out of galvanized steel, but I prefer those that are powder coated. (Powder coating is a way the paint is electrostatically attached to the metal. These typically last much longer than the galvanized cages). Would I take a galvanized cage if it met the shape and wire gauge criteria? Yes, but not till after I could not find the powder coated ones.

Even though they are usually more expensive, cages with Shape A, heavier gauge wire, and the powder-coating are the cages that I look for. They will last much longer than the alternative

Look for Shape A, heavy gauge wire, powder-coated cages. They will last much longer than the alternative!

Tomato Cage Usage

Figure 7.1

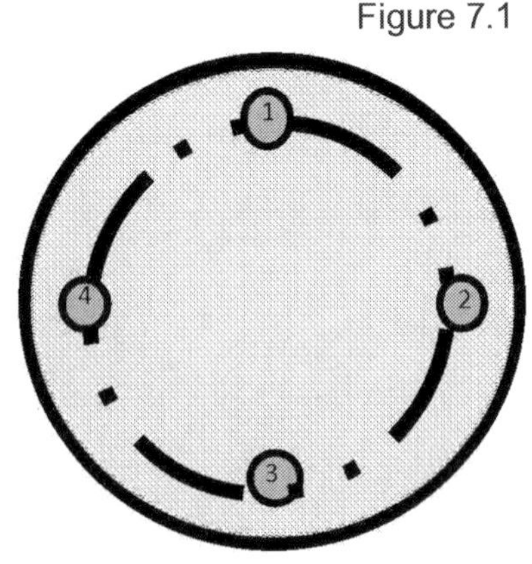

Untrained plants tend to grow all over the place and by default you lose part of your 3D effect. Having said that, it is important to understand how to train the plants. The cage has to be small enough in circumference to fit *inside* the container you are using. If you remember the planting chart from way back in Chapter 1, the cups are placed near the outside of the container (Figure 7.1). This allows the cage, (represented by the dotted line in Figure 7.1) to be placed directly over the plants so that the veggies will be able to grow up on the OUTSIDE of the cage (Pictures 9 & 10). This is very important! Growing up the on the outside allows more room for your plants to reach their full potential. Use twist ties or Velcro strips to attach your plants as they grow up the outside of the cage. Forget to do this, and they will just fall over the edge of the container, thereby taking away one of your levels, and encouraging slugs/snails to eat the produce that is now sitting on the ground.

As for the height of the cage, the variety of tomato will help determine that. Determinate tomatoes are usually shorter plants, while indeterminate tomatoes can get quite tall. I use the tallest Shape A cages I can find when I am planting the indeterminate tomato types.

Picture #9

Picture #10

Train your taller, warm season plants, like tomatoes, eggplants, and peppers to go up the OUTSIDE of the cage!

Picture #11

Trellis

Another great use for cages is as a trellis. With a bit of training, you can use them to keep cucumbers, watermelons, and squash off the ground (Picture 11). This not only keeps the vegetables up and away from pesky insects like slugs, but it also allows those ready for harvest to be seen more readily - making the harvest so much easier. In my opinion, there's nothing more disheartening than finding old, yellow cucumbers that are past their prime because they were hidden in a mess of vines and were not found in time. A trellis can help with that. Not to mention being easier on your back.

Soil Thermometer

Although not absolutely necessary, I have found that having a soil thermometer helps me know when the soil is warm enough to start seed germination. There are several on the market, and like everything else, you get what you pay for. The bigger the face, the easier they are to read. I have also put meat thermometers to good use (Picture 12).

Once the soil gets warm enough to start adding warm season plants, the soil thermometer can be put away till the next season, but I usually end up leaving mine in till I take off the SolarCaps®. It's just nice to be able to check what the soil temperature is at a glance.

Picture #12

Q & A

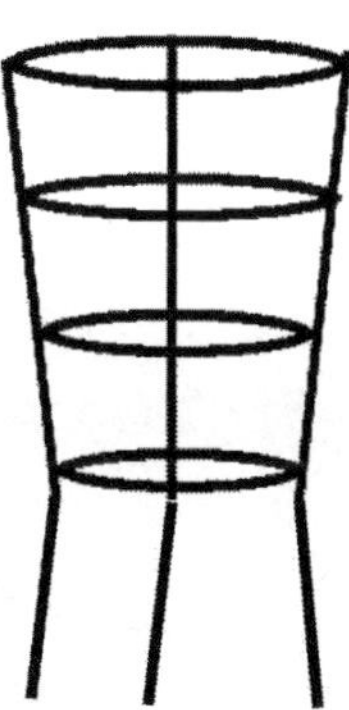

What if I can't find a Shape "A" tomato cage...what then?

Then I would buy the heaviest gauge wired Shape "B" I could find. There are some out there. Once home, I would try prying the legs out a little bit to give it as much stability as you can. When growing plants up the outside of the cage, try to keep the sizes of the plants as evenly matched as possible or the extra weight of one plant may cause it to tip over.

You mention growing the plants up the "outside" of the cage. How is this possible?

Of course, the first item of business is placing the plants on the outer edges of the container, otherwise it will be a challenge to do this. Put in the cage while the plants are still young. ***Don't wait till they get so big you cannot get the cage into the soil because of all the vegetative growth.*** I promise - you will break stems doing this. As mentioned, use twist ties or Velcro tape to attach bigger stems to the outside of the cage as the plant gets bigger. Remember: you are in control and can make the plants go where you want. For really tall indeterminate tomatoes, you will need taller cages or plan on keeping the plant pruned back.

Where can I find these SolarCaps?

You can check with your local independent garden center, farm supply store, or you can go online to containicus.com.

"We hope that, when the insects take over the world, they will remember with gratitude how we took them along on all our picnics."

Bill Vaughn

Chapter 8

Insects & Disease

I am not going to spend a lot of time talking about pests except for some very specific ones because the VERY best way to control disease and insects is to a have a healthy plant, and some pests can be very specific to your location.

Insects

Slugs/Snails

Slugs/snails can be a big deal. They do a great job of breaking down organic matter in the garden, but given the choice they would just as soon eat your vegetables. Wouldn't you? Not only will they eat the vegetation of your cherished plants, but they can damage the actual fruit as well. I had been told my whole life that marigolds were a deterrent to slugs/snails, so imagine my surprise when I planted some into a container and they disappeared overnight! The only thing left was a few disjointed leaves and that familiar slimy trail. Turns out, slugs/snails *love* marigolds! But I've decided I can use this to my advantage. How you ask? If I can entice the slugs to eat a few marigolds before they attack anything else, I win, because then I know I have a problem that needs attention. I would rather sacrifice a few marigolds then have the slugs/snails chewing on my tomatoes and damaging the fruit. So if you see your marigolds disappearing for no good reason, you probably have slugs/snails and need to do something about it - quick. Besides, marigolds can act as a natural deterrent to other insects that want to threaten your vegetables and can add a nice bit of color to the container.

I recommend sticking to the dwarf varieties of marigolds so as not to smother other plants. If you plant the normal sized ones you can cut them back if they get too big.

Slug bait is an option, but some may endanger kids and pets. Sluggo© Snail Bait is an iron phosphate based bait and safe for pets and kids, but I am always on the lookout for organic ways to get the job done if I can.

In that vein, another slug deterrent my dad used to swear by is beer. It seems those slugs/ snails just can't get their fill. Put an empty tuna fish can into the center of your container making sure the top of the can is at soil level. (Think of the cup in a putting green. You don't want any edge sticking up that will stop the slug from going down and in). Add your favorite brew and Waa- la! Your slugs/snails will come to the party, but never go home. (Good thing as we wouldn't want any slugs/snails with a DUI on their record).

Aphids

Aphids are little insects that can show up in many different colors and types. They pierce the epidermis or skin of the plants and suck out the juice. Unfortunately, if you see ONE aphid the likelihood is high that there are MANY of them. When it comes to aphid control, I definitely lean more on the organic side. I would rather let the aphids enjoy my veggies than spray with any pesticide formulation who's residue may end up on my dinner plate. Instead, you can try spraying them off with a high pressure hose or use an organic pesticide like an insecticidal soap.

All other insects that could be a problem can be hand picked off and thrown in the dumpster, so to speak. Remember when I said earlier that my dad sent us out on slug patrol with two wooden slats and we smashed the culprits between the two of them? Same idea.

If you really feel the need to use some form of a pesticide, I would recommend you go for a walk, take a deep breath (Lamaze breathing works great here), then count to ten. Are a few aphids really worth the chance of ingesting something that could make you or your kids sick? One of the benefits of doing this system is that you absolutely KNOW what has or has not been applied as a pesticide. That is something you really don't know when you purchase fruits and vegetables out of the grocery store. For all you know they could have come from other countries. (If you think they have the same EPA laws we do in the USA, you are kidding yourself.) As mentioned above, the worst insecticide I would ever recommend is insecticidal soaps and even then, I just don't think they are necessary.

Diseases

Remember what I said above about healthy plants resisting diseases better than unhealthy ones? Makes perfect sense, right? Did you know that most diseases are caused by improper watering? Mostly of the OVER watering kind. That's an easy fix. You may go to the local garden center and they will probably recommend a fungicide to use, but don't do it. If you are over watering, nothing on the shelf will cure the problem or save the plants. You must change your watering practices (See "Watering," Chapter 5, page 55).

Picture #1

Virus - Some tomatoes are very susceptible to viruses (Picture #1). Unfortunately, there is nothing on the garden center shelf that will fix this. If your plants do come down with a virus, it is better to pull out the infected plants and throw them away before the virus can spread to others. Normally soil born viruses will not be present in soil-less media. If you are concerned, at the end of the growing season, throw that soil away and start over next year.

Mildew - There are two kinds of mildew: downy mildew and powdery mildew. Both appear as grayish blotches on the leaves. One is a nuisance, but the other can be deadly.

Downy Mildew will normally show its self in the early spring when conditions are cool and damp. Make sure there is good air movement around your container and get it into full sun as much as possible. This will usually disappear once conditions improve.

Note!

WHEN USING ANY PESTICIDE ... make sure to read the label and follow all label directions!!!

I cannot stress this enough. Just because it is listed as organic does not mean there are no hidden dangers. Some of the strongest pesticides known to man come from plants and some organic or OMRI listed products can be very detrimental to bees or are made up of fatty acids that you may not want getting into the ground water.

Powdery Mildew can take your plants from this ....to this, before you know it.

Powdery Mildew appears when it is hot and humid and regularly attacks plants like squash and cucumbers. *Ignoring this disease could very well end up in the loss of your plants.* I have seen it kill squash in high desert, low humidity areas so it is a disease that you need to pay attention to. One method of control is to pick off all affected leaves and dispose of them. (Do not attempt to compost infected leaves as the disease can survive in such conditions.) If the infection is too severe do not attempt this method as this would leave your plant denuded. Some have suggested applying a mixture of 1 teaspoon of baking soda to 1 quart of water on a regular basis. Others suggest mixing a crushed clove of garlic with water and spraying. There are also several organic powdery mildew sprays on the market. No matter what method you choose, start spraying once the disease is noticed and keep on top of it.

Weed Control

One of the great advantages of growing in a container in the first place is weeds are virtually non-existent. Newer soil-less mixes should not be weed infested in the first place. As you go through-out the year one or two may pop up. Since you are checking your containers on a regular basis anyway you will notice them while they are still young immature plants, which allows them to be pulled out quite easily. If you have only pulled weeds from a clay soil and not from a soil-less media, you are in for a pleasant surprise.

Note! *Beware! If you let weeds mature and get big in a soil-less media they only come out at a price - lots of soil media and vegetables come out with them.*

"When weeding, the best way to make sure you are removing a weed and not a valuable plant is to pull on it. If it comes out of the ground easily, it is a valuable plant "

Author Unknown

Beware! If you let weeds get big inside the container, they will only come out at a price as they will bring lots of soil with them. The root ball will be massive and you will probably uproot wanted veggies in the process. Keep up with the few weeds you may encounter and your weeding woes and worries will be a thing of the past!

Q & A

You mentioned marigolds and beer as two natural ways to help control slugs. Are there any others?

Sure. I have heard of coffee grinds, egg shells, copper strips, chickens, and as a youth I was part of a slug patrol that was armed with two wooden slats to smash the little critters between them. They can really be a pain. Just know that because we are planting so many plants in such a small space that we are creating the *perfect* environment for slugs/snails… dark, and damp. So you will always need to be on guard, but don't be afraid to try different things. In fact, using many different methods is the best approach. Be persistent and you will get the upper hand.

What are the organic Powdery Mildew sprays available on the market today?

Serenade Garden© has a patented Bacillus subtilis product that will do a nice job. Some recommend Neem oil. Safer© Garden Fungicide is also labeled for Powdery Mildew. No matter what you use, it is best to get a handle on this disease as soon as you see it so that it does not spread throughout the entire plant.

Powdery Mildew

"I believe that virtually everyone has the ability to either grow some food at home, or to find an appropriate location to start a garden. I may sound like a kook who plants my landscape with cucumbers instead of carnations, peppers instead of petunias, and fruit trees rather than ficus, but I am convinced that wherever you go, you can grow food! Now is the time for us to join together and plant the seeds that will transform the places in which we live."

Greg Peterson, *Grow Wherever You Go! Discovering the Place Where Your Garden Lives*

Chapter 9

What To Grow

One can grow just about anything in containers, but here is a list of what I would consider to grow and not to grow. Varieties matter and special consideration needs to be based upon where the crop will be grown. The USDA prints out a hardiness map that lists growing zones (see Appendix). Hardiness zones are used to help gardeners know which plants can grow in their area based upon the average cold hardiness they can survive. Another thing to consider is the time needed to harvest. All vegetable seed catalogs and packets will list the number of days before an actual yield can be realized, which is often referred to as maturity dates or dates to harvest. Of course, maturity dates can be manipulated by the use of season extenders.

Here's a list of what I have personally tried to grow:

Cool Season

Radishes, carrots, spinach, lettuce, swiss chard, chives, beets, chinese cabbage.

Warm Season

Tomatoes, peppers, eggplant, cucumbers, squash, melons, pumpkins, herbs

Here's a list of what I would not try to grow and the reasoning behind it…*but please understand you can try anything you would like. Nothing is out of bounds. Maybe what does not work for me would be perfect for you.*

Corn - The corn plant is very tall and even with good nutrition it usually only gives 1-2 ears per plant. It is the ultimate "it takes up a lot of space without a lot of yield!!" plant. If things in the world drastically change and I decide I need to grow corn, I have a big yard I can tear up and plant. Till then, it's very easy to find corn by the dozen at the grocery store when I get the hankering.

Zucchini - Oh, don't get me wrong. You CAN grow zucchini in your containers. The question is, why would you? The oldest gardening joke around is that if you plant even one zucchini you will be doorbell ditching your neighbors just to get rid of them. Why waste space when you can get them elsewhere very easily.

Broccoli/Cauliflower - I treat these two as the same. Large plants with only one or two heads harvested per plant. In other words, they take up lots of space without a lot of yield. See corn.

Borderline:

Potatoes - Potatoes can be grown very successfully in containers, but they may be the ONLY thing that you grow. The tops will need to get big enough to support the large tubers under the ground, which will limit how many other veggies you will be able to grow as well.

Peas - I have grown peas successfully in containers, but much like potatoes, they want to take up the whole thing. However, because peas can be started so early in the spring, a crop can be grown, harvested, and something else planted before spring is over. It is a nice way to multiply the harvest out of the same container! A SolarCap® works great here.

Seeds Or Transplants

The next big question is whether to purchase seeds or transplants. Here are the pro's and con's of each:

Seeds: The great thing about seeds is you have the world at your fingertips, since you can purchase any seed from just about anywhere on the globe through the internet. Want to try a special variety you've read about? No problem. I start ALL of my cool season vegetables by seed right out in the container. It's easy and I don't have to transplant them. Warm season vegetables are another story and are usually started 6-8 weeks indoors before it is deemed safe to put them outside. The biggest challenge with seeds is having the time, patience and spot in your house that will allow you to grow them. If you only have a north or east facing window, your plants may germinate, but will get leggy from lack of sun. You can compensate, of course, by using artificial lights.

Transplants: Want to plant tomorrow? Start with transplants. Since I struggle with having a good spot to start seeds indoors, I purchase all of my warm season veggies from the local nursery. They come healthy and ready to plant. The challenge here is I am limited to only growing the varieties my local nursery carries. I can shop around, but normally, you will find the same mainstream varieties the nursery knows they can sell. I have seen a resurgence in heritage tomatoes lately, so those are more readily available in my area than they used to be. Yeah! Chances are, the varieties that will do well in your area will be found easily enough, it's just those fun things you want to try that might be hard to find so you may need to resort to finding the seed in catalogs or on the internet instead.

When purchasing warm season plants from the local nursery, make sure to "harden them off" before planting them outside. This means letting them get used to the outside temperature for a couple of days before just plopping them into the container. Not doing so and you will risk losing them before you start.

Seed Catalogs

In an effort to help you decide which varieties of vegetables might work for you, I have perused several seed catalogs and provide their summaries for you here. I consider the seed companies to be the experts, but interestingly enough, they don't always agree.

I have also tried to list where these seeds can be purchased, but please understand that seed companies can change what they offer on an annual basis. Just know that, unless it is patented, if one seed company has it offered, there is a good chance you can find it elsewhere as well…and quite possibly from a source that I don't have listed below.

Burpee Seed - BS	www.burpee.com
Mountain Valley Seed - MVS	www.mvseeds.com
Territorial Seed - TS	www.territorialseed.com
Gurney's Seed & Nursery - GS	www.gurneys.com
Seeds N Such - SS	www.seedsnsuch.com
Johnny's Seeds - JS	www.johnnyseeds.com

Please don't email me chastising me for missing your favorite variety of some specific vegetable. There is no way I can represent *all* of the different varieties available from *every* seed catalog here. Nor have I tried *all* vegetables known to mankind. My attempt here is to show the kinds of vegetables I have had dealings with and how many different options there are at your disposal. As gardeners, I truly believe we all live by this rule:

"There are no gardening mistakes … only experiments!"

Jane Kilburn Phillips

So do your own experiments!

But I *would* like to hear from you. If you have a particular variety or idea that you think would work wonderfully well in this system, please let me know. Then we can learn together.

Cool or Warm Season

You can't garden or work out in the yard for very long before realizing that much like night and day, plants fall into roughly two categories - either cool or warm season. We have mentioned this several times already in this book, but it is important enough to cover again, because you will need to understand this basic concept to be a success at growing vegetables. To ignore this is to put all your time and effort at risk. The cool season veggies are those that can tolerate those late spring frosts, and the warm season ones just can't. We have divided the following into those two main groups, and will try to note any exceptions. Since we can start so early in each season with the use of a SolarCap® we will start with cool season varieties.

What makes a plant a cool season one? I have seen the definition of a cool season plant as one that grows best when it is cool. Well duh. I think a better definition is this; a cool season veggie is one that can germinate while soil temperatures are around 40-45° F and can survive and even thrive in light frosts.

Cool Season

The great thing about cool season vegetables is that when we use any kind of a season extender (like a SolarCap®), we can start them so dang early! But this also means you need to start thinking about your seed needs much, much earlier than you may be used to…like right after Christmas, depending on where you live, because you can start planting in January/February. I think I still shock my neighbor's when they see me outside planting my containers while there is still snow on the ground! I know they think I'm crazy - until I show them radishes that are ready to eat before Easter! Many cool season plants just need a soil temperature of around 40-50° F to germinate. This is easy to achieve with a SolarCap® in place. Once up and covered, they will slowly grow as the weather and sun allow. A hard freeze (0-15° F) may kill really young seedlings and anything from 20-30° F may set them back a bit, but any light spring frosts will not hurt them. Any cover you can give them in the early season would be a big plus!

Here are some cool season varieties you may find interesting to try:

Varieties are listed by maturity dates. Example: 23 days. Use all maturity dates as a guideline only, as they can be affected by your specific microclimate.

Radishes

Radishes are *always* the first to pop their heads out of the ground in my containers. They are so easy to grow, but also very, very healthy for you. And they taste great either fresh out of the container or in a salad. Since they come on so fast, it is best to plant a few several weeks apart so you are not tempted to leave them on your neighbors doorstep. I prefer long tapered ones over blunt round ones, only because I get more per planting. It is important to keep up with thinning them (i.e. eating them), as they mature to give the slower ones space to fully mature. By planting successively, you can enjoy radishes spring, summer, and fall. Companion plants: Carrots, lettuce, cucumbers, spinach, melons, squash.

Cherry Belle - *23 days.* Bright, cherry red, round to globe shaped. Flesh is crystal white, crisp, mild with short tops. MVS

French Breakfast - *24 days.* Blunt, oblong 3 inch roots are red, shading to white at the tip. Flesh is crisp, white and mildly pungent. Great home variety, but does not store well. *Great* for container growing. MVS, SS,

White Icicle - *28 days.* Slender, tapered root is 4-5 inches long with crisp, mild, white flesh. Big tops can crowd out other plants. MVS, JS

Spinach

Popeye had it right - spinach is one of the healthiest plants for human consumption around. It is easily in the top 5 of every list I have ever seen and like most cool season veggies, it does great in a container. You can get a good crop in the spring and then again in the fall. Spinach tends to bolt (go to seed), in the heat of summer. Companion plants: Radish, eggplant, peas.

Regiment - *37 days.* Big, robust leaves. Tolerant of cooler soils. Strong germination. TS

Tyee Hybrid - *37/45 day.* Mild and tender flavor. One of the most bolt resistant varieties on the market. Upright plants reach 10 inches in height. Very heat-tolerant. MVS, TS, JS

Bloomsdale Long Standing - *45 days.* Heirloom variety with heavy, glossy dark green leaves which are heavily savoyed. Slow to bolt. MVS, TS

Lettuce, Romaine

There are many "lettuces" on the market today. I prefer romaine lettuce for three reasons: 1) being a loose leaf type, I can get more plants in a very small space; 2) I can only harvest a typical "head" of lettuce once, while I get several cuttings from the loose leaf type; and 3) because of their higher chlorophyll content, romaine lettuce is much healthier than the other kinds. Companion plants: Radish, beets, cucumbers, carrots, onion.

Flashy Trout Back - *55 days.* A dark green-leaved romaine splashed with wine-red speckles. Very aesthetically pleasing in the container. TS, JS

Cimmaron - *65 days.* Heirloom romaine produces a ten to twelve inch, deep red head with a good flavor and a crisp texture. MVS

Olga - *65 days.* Olga embodies the best of a butter head and romaine in one delicious lettuce. Large, fleshy lime green leaves. TS

Parris Island Cos - *80 days.* Large, upright, full-bodied head with dark green leaves that are mild and sweet. Reaches 10 inches tall. MVS

Carrots

Many gardeners struggle to grow carrots simply because they have such a hard time getting them to germinate. That's no problem in the *Container Gardening in 3D* system! Because of the soilless media we use, getting carrots to germinate is a breeze, and without the large dirt clods found in most garden soils the carrots are usually not deformed. Companion plants: Radish, tomatoes, lettuce, onion.

Little Finger - *55 days.* Very early carrot grows to 4 inches. Tender, sweet, and can be densely planted. MVS

Chantenay Red Core - *68 days.* 5 to 5 ½ inches. Orange, scarlet color. Heavy yields. MVS

Danvers 126 - *73 days.* Industry standard. 7 to 7½ inches. Tender and very sweet. MVS

Swiss Chard

Not many people seem to know this, but Swiss chard is right next to spinach when it comes to a good healthy vegetable. Not only is it very easy to grow, but it can add such color and highlight to your container! If you have not grown any chard yet, at least give it a try. Companion plants: Tomatoes, onion.

Lucullus - *50 days.* Large heavily savoyed green leaves with celery-like white stalks. Grows about 28 inches high. Fine mild flavor. MVS

Bright Lights - *55 days*. 1998 AAS WINNER. A vibrant new Swiss Chard. Distinguished by stems of many different colors - gold, pink, orange, purple, red, and white. Attractive in all stages of growth. Vigorous and widely adapted. Milder taste than ordinary chard. MVS, BS, JS

Rhubarb - *55 days.* Dark reddish-green, heavily crumpled leaves, beautiful crimson stalks and veins. MVS

Ruby Red - *55 days*. Plant produces good yields of dark green shiny leaves with ruby red stalks and veins. Excellent for salads and steamed with others greens. Plant yields all summer long into the fall. MVS

Fordhook Giant - *50 to 60 days*. Broad, dark-green, heavily crumpled leaves with white veins. Leaves are 24-28 inches with 2½ inch thick white stalks. Abundant crops all season and even after the first light frosts. MVS

Rainbow Mixture - *60 days.* A blend of colored chards including red, yellow, orange, white, and vivid pink stems that merge into dark green savoyed leaves. Slow to bolt and quite lovely in bunches. Ornamental/edible landscaping at its best. MVS

Beets

I really hate to admit this, but I have tried to grow beets several times in my containers and have only had mediocre results. So much so, that now I only grow them for beet greens. It may just be the varieties I have been trying, so if you want beets, please give it a shot. Getting them to germinate has never been the problem; getting big beet roots is the challenge. Companion plants: Onions, lettuce.

As one might expect, our definition for warm season vegetables is exactly the opposite of our cool season ones; these plants need warmer soil temperatures to germinate (65-75° F), and even light frosts can heavily damage or even kill the plant.

Warm Season

Tomatoes

Tomatoes are by far the most popular vegetable for home gardeners and with good reason: there is nothing like that first bite into a big, delicious tomato that says summer is really here.

Tomatoes break down into two main areas: determinate or indeterminate. You should choose your variety based upon which category suits you best.

Determinate vs. indeterminate.

Determinate tomatoes are often called bush tomatoes. They are shorter in height than indeterminate varieties and are often thought of when considering container gardening. They also tend to fruit all at the same time so are great if you intend to do some canning. You can get away without tomato cages, but I use them anyway.

Indeterminate tomatoes are also known as 'vining' tomatoes. They tend to grow tall and once they start fruiting, they fruit till frost. Not normally thought of as candidates for containers, I have had good success within the Maximus Containicus Horticus system, but a sturdy tomato cage is a must!

Heirloom vs. Hybrid

Heirlooms are tomatoes from the past that were very popular in their time. Many would consider Heirloom tomatoes better tasting than the newer hybrids, but they also may not be as disease resistant as the newer hybrids and can be quite misshaped.

Hybrid tomatoes have been bred to meet certain specific categories, i.e. disease resistance, sizing, coloring, harvest dates, etc. Some think all of this hybridization comes at the expense of good taste.

Ultimately, all of us will need to judge what we are looking for in a tomato and grow accordingly. Luckily there are enough varieties now available that we could spend the rest of our lives experimenting with several new ones each year.

Tomatoes are known to be heat lovers, but only to a point. They will stop setting fruit when the daytime temperature gets from 85-90° F and the evening temperature is 75° F, or so. If you have a partially shaded patio area, you can try moving your containers so that they do not get so hot in the heat of the day during this time. Companion plants: Carrots, chive, cucumber, lettuce.

Determinate Varieties

Glacier - *55 days.* Orangey red 2 inch tomatoes. Very early producer. TS

Beaver Lodge Slicer - *55 days.* Good productivity, size, quality, and flavor. TS

Oregon Spring - *58–65 days*. Sets fruit early in cool weather. Excellent flavor. MVS, TS.

Northern Delight - *65 days.* Bred to perform in short seasons. Plum shaped fruits. TS

Hamson - *70 days.* Large, deep red fruits. Sets fruit at extreme temperatures. MVS

Keepsake - *70 days.* Tremendous yields. Crisp texture. Outstanding flavor. MVS

Patio Hybrid - *70 days.* Produces 3 to 4 oz. fruit on compact plants. MVS

Siletz - 70-75 days. One of the best slicing tomatoes around. 4-5 inch fruit. TS

Celebrity Hybrid - *72-95 days.* AAS Winner. Med., firm fruits. Crack resistant. MVS, TS

Gill's All Purpose - 75-80 days. Great for canning, juicing, slicing, fresh eating. TS

LaRoma III Red - *76 days.* Very prolific. Large 5 to 8 oz. Disease resistant. MVS

Rutgers - *80 days.* High yields. An exceptional fine mild flavor. Medium-large. MVS

Viva Italia Hybrid - *80 days.* Roma type. High sugar content. High-yielding. MVS

VR Moscow - *80-90 days.* Old fashioned tomato flavor. Outstanding canner. MVS

Indeterminate Varieties

Early Girl Hybrid - *60 days.* Very flavorful, heavy producer throughout season. MVS, TS

Stupice - *60-65 days.* Cold tolerant. 2 inch fruit. TS

Champion II Hybrid - *62 days.* Bred especially for sandwiches. High yields. MVS

Goliath Hybrid - *65 days.* Luscious flavor, blemish-free exterior. Disease resistant. MVS

Thessaloniki - ***68 days.*** Resistant to sunburn, cracks and spots. Pleasant, mild flavor. MVS

Better Boy Hybrid - ***70 days.*** Produces large, red, deep globe shaped fruit. MVS

Momotaro - ***70 days.*** Has won several taste tests. Large slicers. Heat tolerant. TS

Super Fantastic Hybrid - ***70 days.*** Excellent yields over a long season. MVS, TS

Jet Star Hybrid - ***72 days***. Bright red fruits, low acid, free from cracks and scars. MVS

Lemon Boy - ***72 days.*** Unique, lemon yellow skin. MVS

Big Beef Hybrid -***73 days.*** AAS Winner. Extra large fruits. Exceptionally fine flavor. MVS

Heinz - ***75-80 days.*** Early maturing tomato. Cold tolerant. TS

Roma - ***76 days.*** Excellent yields. Popular for cooking, canning, and paste. MVS

Delicious - ***77 day.*** Excellent for salads, tomato juice, and canning. Crack Resistant. MVS

Burpee Big Boy Hybrid - ***78 days.*** Heavy producer. Large, thick walled, meaty. BS, MVS

Husky Red Hybrid - ***78 days.*** Compact upright plants. Dwarf habit. MVS

Beefmaster Hybrid - ***80 days.*** Bears very large, meaty, often over one lbs. in weight. MVS

Rio Grande - ***80 days.*** Excellent for sauces, purees and juicing. extreme temperatures. MVS

Super Marzano - ***85 days.*** High in pectin gives natural creamy thickness to sauces. TS

Golden San Marzano - ***85 days.*** Great for saucing, golden color. TS

Beef Steak (Ponderosa Red) **-*****90 days.*** Large, meaty. Great slicer. MVS

Heirloom Tomatoes

Heirloom tomatoes are in their own non mainstream world. Groomed for taste, these have been chosen for their great flavor and because heirloom tomatoes are not hybridized, you can keep the seeds from year to year.

Manitoba - 66 days. Developed to ripen during short summers. Bears 3-4 inch great tasting fruit. Great for slicing or canning. **Determinate.** TS

Persimmon - 80 days. Really good tasting. Big, beefsteak size fruit. **Indeterminate.** TS

Mr. Stripey - ***80 days.*** Heavy producer of yellow plum-sized fruit with pink stripes on **indeterminate** vines. Low acidity. Makes a great slicer. MVS

Cherokee Purple - ***80 days***. Popular heirloom tomato known for its unusual looks and remarkable flavor. The fruits are large (twelve to sixteen ounces), dark pink with darker purple shoulders. Excellent complex flavor, slight sweet aftertaste, a perfect slicer for tomato sandwiches! **Indeterminate.** MVS, TS, JS

Amish Paste - ***85 days.*** Meaty fruits are juicy and have outstanding flavor, good for sauces or fresh eating. **Indeterminate.** MVS, JS

Brandywine Pink - ***90 days.*** Beefsteak type. Produces large (up to 1 pound), pink fruit. Well known for its excellent, exotic flavor, soft texture, rough shoulders, and creamy smooth flesh. **Indeterminate.** MVS, TS, BS

Cherry Tomatoes

Bite sized explosions of flavor are what make cherry tomatoes so popular. Since they can be used in salads, side dishes, or eaten right off the bush these little wonders are irresistible. Many of these varieties work quite well in containers.

Bitonto - 55 days. Extremely compact, produces masses of 1 inch fruit. **Determinate.** TS

Cherry Buz - ***55 days.*** Produces throughout the whole summer. **Indeterminate.** TS

Sugary - ***60 days.*** AAS Winner. Half-ounce dark pink fruit. ***Semi-indeterminate***. MVS

Juliet Hybrid - ***60 days.*** AAS Winner. Expect high yields. ***Indeterminate.*** MVS, BS

Sun Sugar Hybrid - ***62 days.*** Sweetest tomato available? ***Indeterminate.*** MVS

Sun Gold - 65 days. This is my all time favorite cherry tomato so far! ***Indeterminate***. BS

Yellow Pear - ***70 days.*** Mild-flavored, yellow. ***Indeterminate.*** MVS

Super Sweet Hybrid - ***70 days***. Very high vitamin C content. ***Indeterminate***. MVS

Grapette Hybrid - ***75 days.*** Smaller, gourmet-type tomatoes. ***Semi-determinate***. MVS

Large Red Cherry - ***75 days.*** Excellent flavor over extended season. ***Indeterminate***. MVS

Red Pear - ***78 days.*** Good for canning and sauce. ***Indeterminate.*** MVS

Tomatillo

Do you like salsa? Then these are for you. Treat them like tomatoes and you will have no problem growing them. They can get big and wild, so staking is recommended.

Grande Rio Verde (Husk Tomato) **-** ***80 days.*** Large fruited tomatillo with sweet green fruits measuring 2 to 3 inches across (1.8 - 2.8 oz.), enclosed in a papery husk. Vigorous prostrate vine. It can be used in salsa verde or in pies. Good disease resistance. MVS

Egg Plant

Eggplants do quite well in containers. Many new varieties are now available that are also very aesthetically pleasing.

Fairy Tale Hybrid - ***50 days.*** AAS Winner. New miniature, non-bitter eggplants. The petite plant reaches only 2½ feet tall and wide and adapts well to container gardening. MVS

Gretel Hybrid - ***55 days***. AAS Winner. This new eggplant is extra early and compact. Adaptable to container growing. MVS

Hansel Hybrid - ***55 days***. AAS Winner. New, compact eggplant produces tender, non-bitter fruit that form true miniature sizes - 2 to 6 inches in length. MVS

Long Purple Italian - ***75 days.*** Heirloom classic. Produces club shaped fruit that are 10 inches long by 2 inches in diameter. Each plant will produce four or more dark, purple fruits. MVS

Black Beauty - ***80 days***. Fruits are a deep-purple, egg-shaped globe about 6 by 5 inches. Flesh is smooth, creamy and pale yellow. MVS

Cucumber

Cucumbers work great in a container as they can spill out over the side and take up space not used by other veggies. There are many bush types now on the market, but since you let them trail over the edge, this is not such a concern. Look for varieties that are resistant to powdery mildew. Companion plants: Radish, carrots, beets, tomatoes.

Pickling

Bush Pickle - ***50 days.*** This bush type pickler has a shorter growing season and is perfect for small gardens or containers. Produces fruits that are 4-5 inches long. MVS

Boston Pickling - ***52 days.*** Smooth, bright green, 3 inch fruits have black spines. Very high yields. Bears continually if kept picked. MVS

Wisconsin SMR - ***65 days***. Black spined, blocky, slightly tapered fruits. Very productive. A popular variety. MVS

Lemon - ***65 Days***. Sunny yellow fruits with white flesh resemble a lemon. Has mild, sweet flavor. Use for slicing and pickling. Pick when young. One of my personal favorites. MVS

Slicing

Sweeter Yet Hybrid - ***48 days.*** Dark green fruits are totally non-bitter, and very mild flavored. Vigorous, semi-determinate plants are loaded with strong disease resistance. MVS

Burpless #26 Hybrid - ***50 days.*** Dark green, straight cucumbers to 1 inches long. Good for fresh market & trellised garden. MVS

Sweet Success Hybrid - ***54 days.*** AAS Winner. 14 inches long, straight fruits are very mild, sweet, and seedless if grown away from other varieties. MVS

Diva Hybrid - ***58 days.*** AAS Winner. High yields, superior eating qualities, multiple disease resistances. Fruits 6-8 inches long. Crisp texture, sweet taste, and non-bitter flavor. MVS

Burpee II Hybrid - ***60 days.*** Dark green with white spines, fruit about 8 inches long by 2½ inches across. Cool, crisp flesh and great flavor. MVS

Spacemaster 80 - ***60 days.*** 7½ to 9 inch blocky fruits on dwarf 18 to 24 inch vines. Good flavor -- never bitter. Adapted to a wide range of climates. MVS

Fanfare Hybrid - ***63 days.*** AAS Winner. Uniform, slim fruits are 8 to 9 inches long, flavorful and very attractive. Semi-dwarf plants and very good disease resistance/tolerance. MVS

Oriental Express Hybrid - ***64 days.*** Spineless fruits 10 to 14 inches long. This mild, oriental-type hybrid is ideal for the home garden. MVS

Ashley - ***65 days***. Medium, vigorous vines produce uniform 7-8 inch fruits that have a slight taper on the stem end. Produces heavily in hot, humid areas. Downey mildew resistant. MVS

Marketmore Hybrid - ***67 days.*** Fruits are 8 to 9 inches long, 2½ inches across. Smooth, and dark green. Very popular and productive variety. MVS

Armenian Yard Long - ***68 days.*** Mild flavored, light green fruits can grow to enormous lengths, but are best when harvested at 5 to 7 inches. MVS

Peppers

There are many different kinds of peppers that fall under this tittle, i.e., sweet vs. hot. All work well in containers. I have heard the phrase "peppers like a family". I find this is true; they do quite well when one container is full of nothing but peppers. Because of this, I no longer try to grow peppers with tomatoes; I just grow many peppers together in a single container. Sometimes I will add a level 3 plant that will weep *over* the edge to the pepper containers and they seem to do okay. Companion plants: I am sure there are some, I just don't have experience to recommend any here.

Sweet Pepper Varieties

North Star Hybrid - ***60-65 days.*** Extra early variety for short season areas. Sets fruit under adverse conditions. Peppers average 4 by 3½ inches. MVS

Gypsy Hybrid - ***62 days***. AAS Winner. Huge yields of yellow to orange-red, fruits on a compact plant. 4 to 5 inch long peppers. Sweet and tasty. Resistant to Tobacco Mosaic Virus. MVS

Chocolate Beauty - ***67-70 days.*** Sweet, non-pungent variety bears deep brown, 3½ by 4½ inch fruit. Performs and has the habit of bell types. Tobacco Mosaic resistant. MVS

Red Beauty Hybrid - ***68 days.*** An early, prolific variety bearing very sweet peppers with thick walls. Matures from green to vivid fire-engine red. Tobacco Mosaic resistant. MVS

Bell Boy Hybrid - ***70 days.*** AAS Winner. Compact, sturdy, and productive. Fruits are thick -walled, mostly four- lobed, blocky, and dark green. Resistant to Tobacco Mosaic Virus. MVS

Blushing Beauty Hybrid - ***72 days***. AAS Winner.. Thick, meaty fruits. Compact habit makes this an ideal container pepper. Hearty plants and abundant fruits. MVS

Giant Marconi - ***72 days*** AAS Winner. Best in class for earliness, yield, pepper size, and flavor (sweet, smoky flavor). Resistant to Potato Virus and Tobacco Mosaic Virus. MVS

Jupiter - ***72 days.*** Consistently produces heavy yields. Great for stuffing, freezing, or fresh market. Tolerant of Tobacco Mosaic Virus. MVS

Big Bertha Hybrid - ***73 days.*** Very large 4 lobed fruits can reach 7 inches long and 4 inches across. Vigorous plant gives good cover. Resistant to Tobacco Mosaic Virus. MVS

California Wonder TMR - ***75 days.*** Large yields of blocky, mostly 4 lobed, thick-walled fruit that is mild and sweet. Resistant to Tobacco Mosaic Virus. MVS

Golden Cal Wonder - ***75 days***. 4½ inch blocky, 4 lobed, deep gold colored fruit with good flavor, thick walls, and heavy yield. Sturdy vigorous plants. MVS

Yolo Wonder L - ***75 days.*** Large 4½ by 4 inch, 3 to 4 lobed, glossy peppers on large, sturdy plants. An improved California Wonder. Resistant to Tobacco Mosaic Virus. MVS

Super Heavy Weight - ***77 days.*** Biggest, thickest walled, sweetest blocky bell pepper ever. Matures from green to gold. Marvelous flavor. Resistant to Tobacco Mosaic Virus. MVS

Jumper Hybrid - ***80 days***. Extra big, thick walled pepper. The color turns from medium-dark green to shiny yellow. This one is a showstopper. MVS

Sweet Red Cherry - ***85 days.*** Slightly oblate fruits are 1 to 1½ inches in diameter. Use either red or green, for pickling or in salads. MVS

Pimento L - ***95 days.*** Large, 4½ by 3 inch, heart-shaped peppers with very thick walls. Strong upright plant. Turns bright red at maturity. Resistant to Tobacco Mosaic Virus. MVS

Hot Pepper Varieties

Mariachi Hybrid - ***65-68 days.*** AAS Winner. 'Mariachi' won due to superior fruit size, improved earliness, marvelous yield, and unusually fine flavor. MVS

Tam Jalapeno - ***67 days.*** The flavor of a regular jalapeno without as much bite. Fruits are tapered with a blunt end, 2½ inches long. Plants are not as large as standard jalapeno. MVS

Mucho Nacho - ***68 days.*** A new jumbo jalapeño great for stuffing. The 4 inch long fruits are a mild jalapeno with a fine flavor. Superior yield potential and disease resistant. MVS

Cayenne Long Red - ***70 days.*** 5 inch long fruits are fiery hot, often curled and twisted. Great for drying, processing, or sauces. MVS

Hungarian Yellow Wax Hot - ***72 days.*** Early and prolific, waxy yellow peppers ripening to orange-red. 5 to 6 inch long fruits. Fairly hot. Use for drying, processing, or sauces. MVS

Garden Salsa Hybrid - ***73 days***. A medium pungent chili pepper perfect for salsa. Vigorous hybrid plants have tremendous yield potential. Resistant to Tobacco Mosaic Virus. MVS

Jalapeno M - ***73 days***. Slightly larger fruit and taller plant than early jalapeno above, this heavy yielding pepper will produce over a long period. MVS

NuMex Big Jim - ***75 days***. Mildly hot chile peppers ripen from light green to bright red. Very high yield. Ripens all at once. MVS

Super Chili - *75 days.* AAS Winner. Not unusual for a single plant to produce as many as 300 peppers. Can be used fresh or dried. 35 to 40 thousand SC. MVS

Ancho Grande - *76 days*. Called Poblano when green. Plants are 30 to 36 inches high. A medium hot chile. Continuous harvest. MVS

Anaheim Chili - *80 days.* Milder than some, these meaty chilies are 6 to 8 inches long on 28 to 34 inch plants. MVS

Pasilla Bajio - *80 days.* Mildly hot and slightly sweet. Unique rich flavor that is used in 'mole' and other Mexican dishes. Often called Chilaca when green. MVS

Red Cherry Hot - *80 days*. Very hot, 1-1¼" fruits are nearly round. Walls are medium thick, dark green turning red. Continuous fruiting over a long season. MVS

Santa Fe Grande - *80 days.* These 3½ by 1½ hot peppers turn from yellow to orange-red. The 2 foot plant bears continuous, heavy crops. Resistant to Tobacco Mosaic Virus. MVS

Serrano Chili - *80 days.* A very pungent pepper. The plant grows 30 to 36 inches tall and bears thin-walled, 2 inch, slender fruits. Prolific and ever bearing. MVS

Tai Dragon - *80 days.* Hot little peppers are as ornamental as they are delicious. Grow in the garden or in pots or widow boxes. Around 60 thousand on the Scoville scale. MVS

Holy Mole Hybrid - *85 days.* Used to make molé sauce. The flavor is nutty and tangy. Mature plants can get 3 feet tall. This hybrid exhibits resistance to Tobacco Mosaic Virus. MVS

Habanero - *90 days.* Incredibly hot, small, golden-orange, lantern-shaped fruits. Prefers warm moist conditions. Handle this one with extreme care! MVS

Pumpkin

It seems pumpkins are the new super food! Who knew? Many new varieties of pumpkins are on the market, from very large to very small. It will just depend on how much extra space you have around the container. Make sure you allow for the vines to spread, but the vines are easily trained or pruned to fit your space allowance. Companion plants: Squash.

Sugar Pie - *85 days.* Small, round to somewhat flattened 7-10 inch pumpkins with sweet, fine-grained, yellow flesh flavored for pies and canning. Stores well. MVS

Autumn Gold Hybrid - *90 days.* AAS Winner. Vigorous vine produces 3-5 beautiful pumpkins weighing 7-10 lbs. each. Multi-purpose pumpkin for carving, cooking, and seeds. MVS

Orange Smoothie Hybrid - *90 days.* 5-8 lb. pumpkins. Semi-determinate habit requires less garden space, excellent for painting, carving and makes good pies too. MVS

Baby Boo - *95 days.* A miniature white pumpkin 2-3 inches in diameter by about 2 inches high. Harvest before full maturity as the color will turn a pale yellow when fully ripe. MVS, TS

Jack Be Little - *95 days.* Deep orange fruits are 2 inches tall by 3 inches across. Edible pumpkins are used mainly as fall decorations. Excellent keeper when cured properly. MVS, TS, SS

Lumina - *95 days.* A medium-sized, 10 to 15 pound, white pumpkin with thick orange flesh, excellent for cooking. Fun and different for carving or painting. Stores well. MVS

Wee B Little - 95 days. AAS Winner. True miniature orange pumpkin. Grows to a totally unique size of 8-12 oz. Perfect for interior fall decorations. Can grow from seed. Spreads to 6-8 feet. MVS

Cinderella - *95 to 150 days*. Classic 'Cinderella's Coach' pumpkin. One of the best baking pumpkins, the sweet thick flesh has a better flavor than most carving types. MVS

Lil' Pum-Ke-Mon - *100 days.* The 1-2 lb. fruit is set on a compact vine that offers top yields and easy harvest. MVS

Baby Bear - *105 days.* AAS Winner. Golden-orange flesh is fine for pie making. Semi-hull -less seeds are tasty roasted. Disease-resistant, frost-tolerant vines yield 20 fruits apiece. MVS

Jack O' Lantern - *110 days.* 10 pound fruits are thick walled, and smooth skinned, round to slightly oblong. Thick flesh is fine for cooking, but really shines as a carving pumpkin. MVS, SS

Squash

There are many kinds of squash: summer, winter, zucchini, gourds. All work. Much like pumpkins and melons, just make sure you have **lots** of room around the container to run the vines, as most in this category will put out lots and lots of vine. Easy to train or prune them depending on your space allowance. Companion plants: Radish, melon, cucumbers.

Melons

Like squash, there are many different types of melons: cantaloupe, watermelon, crenshaw, and honeydew. Many work. Make sure to leave lots of room for the vines to spread. Look for varieties that are resistant to powdery mildew. Companion plants: Radish, cucumbers, squash.

Beans

I have never tried beans, pole or bush, and not for reasons most folks may think. I know they would work, but I just don't like beans in any form, so I choose not to grow them. Remember I said, "only grow the things you will eat"...otherwise, it's just a waste of space. If I did grow beans, I would choose pole beans and train them up a very tall tomato cage. Seed them directly into the container, but wait a little longer into the spring than other directly seeded veggies. Frosts will have a higher chance of stunting or killing beans than other cool season plants. Companion plants: Radish, cucumbers, egg plant, Swiss chard, carrots, beets.

Herbs

Like all plants I consider for container gardening, size, growth habit, potential yield, and possible companion benefits all make a difference. Many herbs work well in containers, but some are very hard to start from seed, so buy plants at the local garden center or nursery. Below is list of just a few.

Basil - Fairly easy to grow, and is worth trying. Can start from seed or purchase transplants. Basil prefers heat so all seeds will need to be started indoors at least 90 days before transplanting them outside. Do not over water .

Chives - A great addition to any container because not only do chives thrive, but they can add some benefits as to a natural deterrent for some insects. Can be grown from seed or purchase transplants.

Cilantro - I love just about any dish with cilantro in it, so was excited to try this in a container. I have to admit that I had mixed results. Because cilantro has such a deep tap-root, it is best started by seed inside the container. It grows fast and goes to seed quickly, so you will need to keep up with it.

Dill - There is nothing like the smell of dill in the air. Dill is in the same family as cilantro and presents some of the same challenges when it comes to transplanting, so it is best to sow the seed right into the container. Dill will grow into a large plant, but there have been some dwarf varieties offered on the market lately that would work better in a container.

Mint - This is another very aromatic plant. There are mints of all sizes, shapes, and smells. Mint grows very slowly from seeds, but does quite well as a transplant. It's very hardy and if you are not careful, the mint plant will become the ONLY plant you have in your container.

Oregano - Famous for spicing up Italian dishes, oregano can also be a very attractive container plant. It is susceptible to root rot, so let it dry out between watering's. Usually purchased as a transplant than started from seed.

Parsley - One of my mom's favorite additions to her well known potato salad, parsley can go out early and withstand some light frosts. It is not easy to grow from seed, so look for it at your local nursery.

Rosemary - Rosemary is very slow to germinate and best purchased as a transplant or can be started as a cutting. Like oregano, it has issues with over watering, so a good draining soil is a must.

Stevia - A natural sweetener that is much stronger than sugar with zero calories, stevia is on my list to try in my containers. It may be one of those plants that does not play well with others, but only by trial and error will this be determined.

Thyme - Used in landscapes as well as window boxes, thyme is a crowd pleaser. Very easy to grow in containers. Can be started by seed or purchased as transplants.

Container Gardening in 3D

Appendix

Glossary

AAS - Stands for All America Selections. All America Selections is an independent, non-profit organization that tests new varieties then introduces only the best garden performers as AAS Winners.

Aerobic - The opposite of anaerobic, wherein oxygen is freely exchanged with the root system.

Anaerobic - The absence of free oxygen; which basically means your plants are in a situation where the roots are slowly suffocating to death. Heavy clay soils can be so anaerobic they are blue in color.

Carbon to Nitrogen ratio - Commonly referred to as the C:N ratio is the ratio of the mass of carbon to the mass of nitrogen in a substance. In horticulture it used to determine how fast microbes will break materials down as a higher ratio will result in slower composting rates. A higher ratio also has the potential to use much needed nitrogen to break materials down, thereby stealing it from desired plants causing them to yellow.

Container Gardening in 3D - A system using 3 distinct growing levels to grow vegetables in the container:

1) Down in the soil (radishes, carrots, etc.).

2) Above the container (tomatoes, peppers, etc.).

3) Spreading or weeping down over the edges of the container (cucumbers, melons, etc.).

Companion planting - Plants that not only grow well together, but add synergy or insect protection for one another.

Complete fertilizer - Any fertilizer that has nitrogen, phosphorus, and potassium as part of its makeup...even though there are other major and minor nutrients needed for healthy plant growth.

CRF – An acronym for controlled release fertilizer. It is a fertilizer prill coated with a polymer to slow down the release rate of the main ingredient...usually nitrogen. CRF's are safer to use as there is less chance of burning plants. It allows the user to only fertilize once or twice per year, instead of the every other week regiment water soluble fertilizers demand. As an increased benefit, CRF's are less likely to have any nitrogen running out of the bottom of the container.

Dirt - A mix of clay, loam, sand, and humus in various amounts found in the garden. Typically thought of as the stuff on the bottom of your shoe when you come into the house. *It is not meant for containers.*

Hardening off - The practice of setting plants that originate from inside a greenhouse or home outside for several days and nights so they can acclimate to the swings in temperature.

Intensity/Density planting - Describes pushing the limit on how close plants can be planted together to experience increased yields.

Maximus Containicus Horticus - My motto. A fun term that defines our goal to get the highest yield of produce out of every single container garden.

Mulch - Materials such as decaying leaves, bark, compost or plastic spread around or over a plant to enrich or insulate the soil. Also used as a form of weed control.

pH - pH is a measure of the hydrogen ion concentration of a solution, which basically makes a solution either acidic or basic. All plants have a preferred pH range they like to grow in. pH also can affect which nutrients are available to plants.

Potting soil - A pre-mixture of different raw materials like peat, bark, coir, perlite, vermiculite and nutrients meant to be used as a growing medium for plants in containers.

Salts - When we talk about salts in soils, it is a bad thing. Salts can build up and disrupt the plant roots ability to take in water, thereby mimicking drought symptoms. They can build up due to the constant use of synthetic fertilizers or be present in manure composts. No matter the source, flushing the container with clear water when watering can help reduce the amount of salts found in soils.

Savoyed - Curly & wrinkly. Usually used in descriptions about plant leaves.

Soil-less media - A growth media not containing dirt or garden soil. Usually made up of peat, bark, coir, perlite, vermiculite or other raw materials, and meant to be used as a potting soil.

SolarCap® - greenhouse-like covers that cover the entire container and allows you to start planting earlier in the spring.

Succession Planting - Planting crops more than once per year to increase potential yields.

Two or more crops in succession...after one crop is harvested, another is planted in the same space. The length of the growing season, climate, and crop selection are key factors. For example, a cool season spring crop could be followed by a heat-loving summer crop or same crop.

Successive plantings...several smaller plantings are made at timed intervals, rather than all at once. The plants mature at staggered dates, establishing a continuous harvest over an extended period. Lettuce, radishes, spinach, and other salad greens are common crops for this approach.

Top dress – (top dressing) a layer of bark, compost or other organic materials that are meant to stay on the surface of the soil and not meant to be plowed in or tilled.

Xeric - Containing little moisture or dry. Can be used in reference to landscaping that plans on little water being applied by sprinkler.

Planting Chart

Vegetables	Plant Spacing for 3D Containers	Best Starting Method	Germinating Soil Temps	pH	Days to Emergence	Weeks before Transplanting	Succession Planting

Hardy Cool Season Veggies

Arugula	3-4"	Direct Seed	45-70° F	6.0-7.5	2-15	N/A	Yes
Beets	3-4"	Direct Seed	45-60° F	6.0-7.5	5-17	N/A	Yes
Carrots	1-2"	Direct Seed	50-75° F	6.0-7.5	6-21	N/A	Yes
Radish	1-2"	Direct Seed	45-75° F	6.0-7.5	4-11	N/A	Yes
Spinach	3-4"	Direct Seed	45-75° F	6.0-7.5	6-21	N/A	Yes
Lettuce - Romaine	3-4"	Direct Seed	40-75° F	6.0-7.5	2-15	N/A	Yes
Swiss Chard	3-4"	Direct Seed	50-75° F	6.0-7.5	5-17	N/A	Yes

Notes:

Any veggie that can germinate at 40-50° F is a candidate for starting under a SolarCap® in the early spring.

Planting Chart

Vegetables	Plant Spacing for 3D Containers	Best Starting Method	Germinating Soil Temps	pH	Days to Emergence	Weeks before Trans-planting	Succession Planting

Warm Season Veggies

Bush Beans	*On the Edge & allowed to grow Up	Direct Seed	50-75° F	6.0-7.5	5-17	N/A	No
Cucumbers	*On the Edge & allowed to weep Over	**Direct/ Transplant	65-80° F	6.0-7.5	5-17	8-10	No
Egg Plant	*On the Edge & allowed to grow Up	Transplant Only	65-80° F	6.0-7.5	5-17	6-8	No
Peppers	*On the Edge & allowed to grow Up	Transplant Only	65-80° F	6.0-7.5	5-17	8-10	No
Tomatoes	*On the Edge & allowed to grow Up	Transplant Only	65-80° F	6.0-7.5	8-25	6-8	No
Tomatillos	*On the Edge & allowed to grow Up	Transplant Only	65-80° F	6.0-7.5	8-25	6-8	No
Pumpkins	*On the Edge & allowed to weep Over	**Direct/ Transplant	65-80° F	6.0-7.5	8-25	8-10	No
Melons	*On the Edge & allowed to weep Over	**Direct/ Transplant	65-80° F	6.0-7.5	8-25	8-10	No
Squash	*On the Edge & allowed to weep Over	**Direct/ Transplant	65-80° F	6.0-7.5	8-25	8-10	No

Notes:

* There will only 3-4 of these per container, but they can mixed and matched., EXCEPT peppers. See page 98.

**I have tried direct seeding some of these, but found transplants work best.

Use the SolarCap® to gets these off to the right start with less transplant shock.

Indeterminate tomatoes, and tomatillos <u>**MUST**</u> be staked.

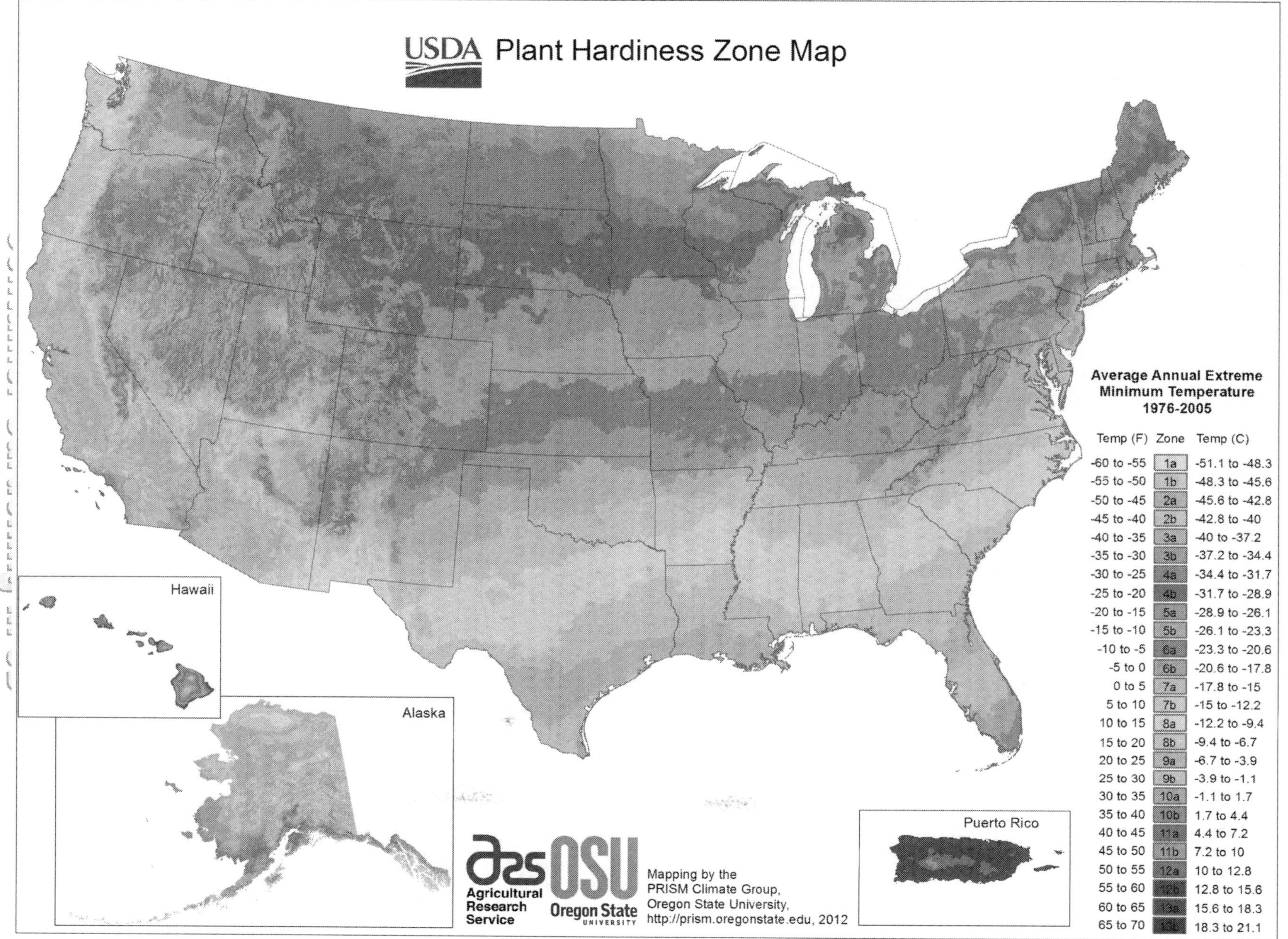
USDA Plant Hardiness Zone Map
Average Annual Extreme Minimum Temperature 1976-2005
Temp (F) Zone Temp (C)
-60 to -55 1a -51.1 to -48.3
-55 to -50 1b -48.3 to -45.6
-50 to -45 2a -45.6 to -42.8
-45 to -40 2b -42.8 to -40
-40 to -35 3a -40 to -37.2
-35 to -30 3b -37.2 to -34.4
-30 to -25 4a -34.4 to -31.7
-25 to -20 4b -31.7 to -28.9
-20 to -15 5a -28.9 to -26.1
-15 to -10 5b -26.1 to -23.3
-10 to -5 6a -23.3 to -20.6
-5 to 0 6b -20.6 to -17.8
0 to 5 7a -17.8 to -15
5 to 10 7b -15 to -12.2
10 to 15 8a -12.2 to -9.4
15 to 20 8b -9.4 to -6.7
20 to 25 9a -6.7 to -3.9
25 to 30 9b -3.9 to -1.1
30 to 35 10a -1.1 to 1.7
35 to 40 10b 1.7 to 4.4
40 to 45 11a 4.4 to 7.2
45 to 50 11b 7.2 to 10
50 to 55 12a 10 to 12.8
55 to 60 12b 12.8 to 15.6
60 to 65 13a 15.6 to 18.3
65 to 70 13b 18.3 to 21.1
Hawaii
Alaska
Puerto Rico
Agricultural Research Service
OSU Oregon State University
Mapping by the PRISM Climate Group, Oregon State University, http://prism.oregonstate.edu, 2012

About the Author

Mathew Jentzsch has been involved in the green industry for over 35 years. After graduating in Landscape Horticulture he worked as an intern at a prominent retail garden center, a landscaper/landscape designer, regional manager of a lawn care company, golf course assistant superintendent, manufacturer's representative for a peat moss company, owner/operator of a landscape maintenance company, and finally, as an inventor/advocate for container gardening.

Mathew is married with 6 kids and lives in Utah.

Container Gardening in 3D

29353663R00063

Made in the USA
San Bernardino, CA
20 January 2016